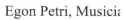Egon Petri, Musici

Egon Petri at home in Oakland, California. The inscription on the reverse of the photograph reads, "To Al—with all best wishes for his future success & happiness / affectionately / Egon Petri / Oakland / July '57."

Egon Petri, Musician to the World

Interviews and Commentary

Alfred Kanwischer

Bibliographical information held by the German National Library

The German National Library has listed this book in the Deutsche Na-
tionalbibliografie (German national bibliography); detailed biblio-
graphic information is available online at http://dnb.d-nb.de.

1st edition - Göttingen: Cuvillier, 2019

© CUVILLIER VERLAG, Göttingen, Germany 2019
   Nonnenstieg 8, 37075 Göttingen, Germany
   Telephone: +49 (0)551-54724-0
   Telefax: +49 (0)551-54724-21
   www.cuvillier.de

   ISBN 978-3-7369-9968-8
   eISBN 978-3-7369-8968-9

Contents

List of Illustrations

Dedicated to
Heidi and Sylvia,
My beloved scribes

Preface

Blessed with a colossal technique and a superabundance of musicianship and intelligence, Egon Petri was one of the supremely gifted pianists of this [20th] century.

Bryan Crimp, 1994

I have long wanted to gather together and share reminiscences of our teacher and friend Egon Petri (1881–1962). A goodly amount of these are in his own words, since in his last year of life I met with him weekly for intimate question-and-answer sessions, using an ancient tape recorder. Throughout, he was ever cordial, generous, frank, and (it still seems to me) utterly truthful. He always spoke with that charming combination of confidence, worldly knowledge, and humility.

It is clear now, in 2018, that Egon Petri's story, his performing and teaching art, are as relevant as ever, an invaluable link from the past to the future. His remarks, mottos, and maxims by no means encompass his artistry and instruction, but they do represent his modes of thinking—arresting, penetrating, sensible, time-independent. He was not only a great twentieth-century virtuoso, but also a great teacher. You will see this for yourself, Dear Reader, and this is fitting: Petri always insisted that his ideas stand on their own.

I have divided this account into four sections: 1. Youth; 2. Influences; 3. Teaching; 4. Repertoire and Performance. In addition to the taped interviews, these chapters also reflect information gathered from personal conversations over the years, as well as materials from private lessons and master classes.

Heidi Elfenbein (my future wife) and I were already studying with Egon Petri when we met. Besides our weekly lessons with him in his home, we performed in his summer master classes at the San Francisco Conservatory and Mills College in Oakland, California. During those years, we experienced the joy of Petri's company socially as well as professionally. Lessons always went overtime. His generosity even included the purchase of music: one day at a lesson, Egon was horrified with Heidi's edition of the Beethoven Sonatas (Schnabel).

"My dear child," he said, "you must go right away to the Berkeley Music House and buy the Tovey edition!" When she replied, "I'll do it soon," Egon immediately added, "Just put it on my account."

Moreover, lessons regularly metamorphosed into social occasions. Dinner would follow, with special attention to the choice of wines. Stories and wit would illumine the night. There seemed no end to the tales of events, persons, places, or bemused speculations over causes, devices, or results. Egon attended a rehearsal for my debut with the San Francisco Symphony (Beethoven's "Emperor" Concerto); the fee allowed Heidi and me to marry. In fact, Egon was best man for our wedding in San Francisco! For us, these were exhilarating times.

We always attended Egon's performances in various locations in the Bay Area. As usual, he played a wide range of literature. Although he was then in his seventies, his concerts retained their vigor, structural acumen, and emotional breadth. This included a performance of the F-minor Quintet of Brahms with the Budapest String Quartet, and, at age seventy-nine, his presentation of the thirty-two Beethoven sonatas in six recitals at the San Francisco Museum of Art. I turned pages for these recitals. Egon seldom looked up or glanced at the score. Several times, as I sat entranced, he rescued me by deftly turning pages back for repeats, a quicksilver smile signalling forgiveness.

Egon seemed always cognizant of what his pupils (and former pupils) were doing. Whenever Heidi and I performed somewhere, he wished to know what, when, where. In our live solo broadcasts over radio KPFA in Berkeley, he always rang up the station at intermission, acknowledging us, urging us on: "Lovely! Go on, go on." He always tuned in and thus helped validate our forays into literature we knew he had performed so brilliantly all over the world. Such generosity seemed singular then. Many decades later, it only seems more rare.

In the 1950s, several of Petri's LP recordings appeared, including a Westminster disc of Liszt transcriptions (Mendelssohn, Gounod, Mozart, Beethoven) and the Mephisto Waltz, an album of Bach-Busoni transcriptions (including Toccata and Fugue in D Minor, and the "St Anne" Prelude and Fugue in E-flat), and a recording of a stunning performance of Beethoven's "Hammerclavier" Sonata. An album of Busoni followed, which included the Fantasia contrapuntistica of which Jan Holcman, in a retrospective in the *Saturday Review* of 25 May 1972, stated, "In this disc Petri's pianism reaches spectacular heights." A Concord disc of late Beethoven sonatas also appeared. The critics proudly proclaimed the "Hammerclavier" Sonata a recording of Petri in his prime. Egon was very pleased, for he said, "How nice! For no one likes to sit on his own tombstone."

After his death in 1962, recordings occasionally surfaced, such as HQM 1112, an EMI reissue of sterling performances from earlier 78s, and a dell'Art disc (DA 9009) gleaned from Petri's radio broadcasts during a six-month residence in Basel, Switzerland. This recording includes Franck's Prelude, Chorale, and Fugue, Liszt's Petrarch Sonnets, and pieces of Medtner and Busoni. The Franck, especially, is a haunting performance, seeming to sum up a lifetime of sorrow, resolve, and triumph. These kinds of epic pieces seemed to suit Egon best.

Lastly, in early 2016, a kind of milestone appeared, a caring, deft remastering of all Petri's Columbia and Electrola solo and concerto recordings from 1929 through 1951, by Appian Publications & Recordings Ltd., UK (APR 7701), on seven discs. Here are the epochal recordings of Petri's performances of Bach, Bach-Busoni, Beethoven, Liszt, Chopin, Franck, etc.—nine hours and one-minute! I comment on this recording set at the end of chapter 4, "Repertoire and Performance" (see the "Postscript" section in chapter 4). Here, I say only that APR has done us an incomparable favor, for now one can hear Egon's unique artistry in new clarity and depth.

A note regarding my taped interviews mentioned at the outset. Alas, the original tapes from 1961 to 1962 no longer exist, due to our nomadic lives, many residencies, and the passage of time. The small portable tape recorder, which recorded via small spools (at 33 1/3 speed), is also no longer extant. It was completely worn out, with the constant forward and backward turning in order to transcribe the text via typewriter, in the years 1962–1963. This acute and punishing process was accomplished almost entirely by a brave Heidi Elfenbein-Kanwischer over many months. Currently in our possession are the transcriptions themselves, almost two hundred pages, legal size, typed, double-spaced: Egon's words exactly as he spoke them.

In addition, we still possess two booklets given us by Egon: one, an alphabetical repertoire list of Egon's programs from 1892 to 1929 (the compiler unknown; see Appendix), and the other, replicas of Egon's concert programs from 1931 through 1936, which show that Egon was concertizing throughout the 1930s in Europe, Great Britain, Scotland, the United States, and Canada. Naturally, I have leaned heavily on these booklets in chapter 4, "Repertoire." These two documents alone, stating the simple facts, are astonishing in their scope and import. When Egon said to his students, "I think a pianist should be able to play everything," he was obviously speaking to himself. To somewhat simplify his code: he expected singular excellence in everything whenever and wherever one performed. That he traversed such an enormous range of literature remains phenomenal.

In my opening paragraph, I mentioned, along with Egon's extraordinary confidence and worldly knowledge, his essential humility. As he said, "I think that I am so chaste a man. . . I don't play to the gallery. I don't like to show the works. If you have a watch . . . you want to see the time . . . and not all the springs inside." "I try not to overshadow the composer."

In short, then, through these years, Egon, who had seen worlds appear and disappear in his epochal life[1], remained always a cheering presence, ever rational, probing, bemused, ironic—kind—a philosophical pragmatist. Happily, he remained for us to the end both a formidable, exacting taskmaster and a generous, encouraging friend. As you will see, his story is as arresting as his art.

Note: It is already obvious that this will be a partisan narrative. Nevertheless, I have endeavored to tell the truth as Egon told it to me.

---

[1] Not only the demise of the Austro-Hungarian Empire, the advent of the First World War, the Russian Revolution, the rise of Franco, Mussolini, the rise and fall of Nazism and Hitler, the rise of Stalin, but also smaller occurrences. Petri told us: "There is also a Russian church which was built in Warsaw on the big Satsky Platz (built by the Prince of Saxony, August the Strong, who reportedly had three hundred illegitimate children, who also became king of Poland). Satsky Platz was the old square in which all the riots were held. The Russians, to spite the Poles, built a church with onion-shaped domes and cupolas on this place. I was in Warsaw when it was Russian, in 1914, just before the war started, still under the Czar (and I played in Moscow and St. Petersburg, the Bach D-minor Concerto, etc.).

"The second time I came, the Germans were there. . . . They were taking what was supposed to be pure gold tiles from the onion domes. (The Russians, who had been in charge of all this, used copper and had just had the gold gilded on it, and thus cheating, they made their money.) The Germans needed metal for shooting, so they melted all these gilded copper plates and made them into bullets. They covered the domes with tin.

"The third time I was there, Poland was free, so they had razed the church to the ground, and there was the old Satsky Platz back again!

"Now, in reality . . . I wouldn't be at all surprised if now (in 1962!), the Russians had again erected a church and the Poles all forced to be Catholic!"

To my entire recollection, Petri did not feel the need to alter, to deceive, to aggrandize. And whether he remembered clearly or not, he always admitted either openly and cheerfully.

Brief biographies of Egon Petri often refer to a "heart attack" he reportedly suffered in 1946, after which he supposedly "abandoned the concert stage for a teaching post in California" (e.g., *Gramophone* review, Dec. 2015). This is not accurate. Petri did not have a heart attack, but rather a gastric attack, according to his physician, Doctor Deissler, a close friend of Petri and his daughter Ulla (who always lived close by). After arriving in California, Petri soon recovered and never abandoned the concert stage. As Ulla said, "If Pater did not play enough concerts, doors would start to slam."

In his later years, Egon was advised by Dr. Deissler to spend one day a week at rest in bed "doing nothing." Petri accepted this cheerfully, saying, "I am to do absolutely nothing, and I have an entire day in which to do it."

On those rest days, Egon's favorite activity was reading Dickens (also a favorite for recital days), or reading full scores of Haydn's symphonies, which he especially prized. (Egon had a complete edition of Haydn's one-hundred-and-four symphonies in his library.) As he said, "Haydn always cheers me. There are always places where I laugh out loud." Petri held Haydn on a par with Mozart, an opinion not generally accepted then.

Egon had personal joys besides Dickens (especially the *Pickwick Papers)* and Haydn: he adored the sweet pea flowers that Mrs. Petri grew in her capacious garden. She always had generous numbers growing in long rows for Egon's delight, and bouquets displayed in their home. Then, too, he held deep memories of the first crocuses peeking up through snow in the mountains surrounding Zakopane, Poland. No matter how often he witnessed the phenomenon, Egon recounted, it always moved him to tears. He prized California, too, "where one can grow so many things year 'round—even music!"

Egon was modest, though confident, as I have said, and for him, truth-telling emanated from a deep innate honesty, fierce integrity as an artist, and his humanity as a world citizen. Nearly sitting on his own tombstone, as he said, he felt even more free to tell the truth just as he held and recalled it. So, he did. And here it is.

Alfred, Heidi, Egon, and Heidi's mother in Berkeley, California, 1962, shortly before Sylvia was born.

Acknowledgements

I thank Jonathan Aretakis for his close, acute copyediting. I acknowledge Michael Schmitz of Cuvillier Press for his endless patience and ever-courteous care. I thank two women in my life who have again proven invaluable: Heidi Kanwischer, by her heroic tape transcription already cited, by her many detailed editings, and penetrating advice; and Sylvia Miller, beloved daughter, by her astute editings and deft superintending of this manuscript through the labyrinthian stages of publication. Both ever tempered profound knowledge with affection. Without them, this manuscript would never have seen print.

If there are any remaining errors in this book, they are mine alone.

Chapter 1

Youth: Violin and Piano

> If ever there was a pianist who used a colossal technique merely as a means to a musical end, it was Egon Petri.
>
> Harold Schonberg, *New York Times*, 10 March 1985

It's best to start as near the beginning as possible: the birth of Egon Petri, on 23 March 1881 in Hanover, Germany.

> The first thing I want to say is that my name is not Italian nor Hungarian. All my ancestors on my father's side are Dutch. I have a book in my possession, The Contributions of Holland to the Sciences, that says there was a very famous mathematician in Deventer in the year 1575 whose name was Kalus Peters, alias Petri. So the name is Latin, because that was the language in which scientists wrote and talked together. . . . So that is the origins of my name—which is Latin and meant "the son of Peter"! I should call myself Peterson, but nobody would know who I am.

About his family on his father's side, he recalled:

> I never knew my grandparents on my father's side. I only know that my grandfather was an oboist, probably in the Utrecht Orchestra. He was born in Geist, a suburb of Utrecht.
>
> I don't know where my father learned to play the violin—probably from a member of the orchestra in Utrecht.

Egon recalled having musical uncles:

My father had three brothers, Martinus, Willem, and Albert. Albert died early of T.B. My two surviving uncles were also excellent musicians. Martinus was an oboist and organist, and Willem was a cellist, violinist, pianist, and theory teacher, who founded the Petri Music School—that existed until my uncle died at eighty-four. I've been in the building very often and practiced there. It was also his home. (The two brothers had homes opposite each other). . . . I had been practicing and eating there when the war broke out in 1939. Willem was the teacher of Willem Mengelberg[2]—the very famous conductor under whom I played very often in the Amsterdam Concertgebouw.

In 1883, the Petri family moved to Leipzig. Egon recalled:

In Leipzig, when I was three years old, I was in Kindergarten. Once my mother had a complaint—the teacher wrote a letter which said, "Will you please tell your son Egon not always to sing in thirds and sixths, because it upsets all the other children." We were supposed to sing in unison, of course. I found it pretty. The first signs of musicality.

Early Music Education and Performances

Egon Petri remembered early lessons with his mother, Kathi, on a quarter-size violin, the first on his fifth birthday. This was a tradition, since she, too, had been given her first lesson at age five, on a quarter-size violin, by *her* father, then second violinist in the Berlin State Opera Orchestra. She came from a distinguished musical German family.

My grandfather was second violinist in the Berlin State Opera. He was not a great violinist—as my father was. My mother had been given a little violin when she was five years old which became a tradition in our family. I was given the same little quarter violin when I

---

[2] See note no. 15 and text later in this chapter for more on Willem Mengelberg.

was five, and got my first lesson from my mother on my fifth birthday, which I think was a very cruel birthday present!

Egon remembers her playing and teaching as she prepared students for eventual lessons with her renowned husband, Henri Wilhelm Petri (1856–1914), a highly gifted professional Dutch violinist.

> My mother was quite a nice violinist, and she gave elementary lessons, prepared pupils for my father later on. She had great difficulty with technical passages, but she was a very good musician.

Egon recalled not only his mother's "large brown eyes," but also her development as a singer, performing for charity events with her husband, often singing her husband's songs. Egon held manifold memories of her "fine mezzo-soprano voice, deep and velvety." Later, Egon said, "I loved to accompany her and loved to hear her sing when I was a boy."[3]

Egon studied the violin with his mother "until about age ten or twelve," when his father, Henri, took over. "Then I really enjoyed myself," Egon declared. His father was a master violinist from Utrecht, Holland, held as one of the most distinguished pupils of his famous teacher, Joseph Joachim (1831–1907), the premier violinist of Europe, lifelong intimate friend of Brahms. By age fifteen, Henri was already an orphan. He subsequently received a scholarship from King Wilhelm III of Holland for study with Joachim in Berlin. A guardian was appointed, and money was sent each month to Berlin.

In Berlin, young Henri boarded with the parents of his future wife. "Early," recalled Egon, "my father was very easy with his money. That I also have inherited." In fact, "my father was very frivo-

---

[3] Early, then, Egon had most personal experiences playing lieder. Regarding the Schubert lieder, Schubert-Liszt arrangements, the Liszt "Petrarch" Sonnets, or Beethoven's "Adelaide," Egon said, "Of course, Alfred, the poetry is the key."

lous and light-hearted, and would pawn his clothes when he wanted extra money. When this was reported to Henri's guardian by his future father-in-law, the guardian would respond, 'Oh, let him pawn his clothes; we'll send him money for new ones.' This seemed so strange to my grandfather [Henri's future father-in-law], who was very economical and hadn't much money."

Egon recounted his parents' early acquaintance. "So, there was my mother as a young girl; my father was fifteen, my mother sixteen. Now, one day my father heard my mother play [on the violin] and saw that technique was a great effort [for her], and so he just took the violin out of her hands and played these passages as a virtuoso, and my mother looked at him with her big, brown eyes—I can see her now, as her portrait is hanging over the piano there—and she admired him, and naturally—well, it ended in falling in love and that is how I came into this world."

During Egon's youth, Henri became in turn concertmaster of the Royal Opera Orchestra in Hanover, then concertmaster of the Gewandhaus Orchestra in Leipzig (made famous by Mendelssohn) in 1883,[4] and finally, concertmaster of the Dresden State Opera Orchestra in 1888. Egon recalled, "My father got an appointment in Hanover one year after they were married—and that is where I was born.

---

[4] Egon told us a revealing story of Arthur Nikisch (1855–1922), renowned Hungarian conductor, premier conductor of the Leipzig Theatre during Henri Petri's tenure in Leipzig. He was known as the first great "conductor-as-hero," so to speak. In conducting the opening of Beethoven's Fifth Symphony, Egon related that "he [Nikisch] played the first eight notes as if they were the whole symphony. . . . Really," continued Egon, "If anyone did that today, they would be laughed out of the concert hall. But at that time it seemed so impressive and so great." Nowadays in the twenty-first century, more of Nikisch might be welcome!

Hanover was very close to Sonderhausen where my father later became concertmaster of the orchestra and the private instructor of the Prince of Sonderhaus. That is also where Liszt and his whole gang came over in 1880. The photo on the wall here is a photo given to my father from Liszt and signed 'Very cordially to Henri Petri,' from F. Liszt.' My mother sang to Liszt as a young married woman."

Of a special kiss, Egon said, "So, young Liszt played to Beethoven, and Beethoven kissed him; then my mother sang to Liszt, and Liszt kissed my mother; then I played for my mother, and my mother kissed me." Although Egon related this episode in a bemused way, it was obvious to us that he revered the connection as representing a precious link to a hallowed—by now, fabled—past, a tradition now personal, whose ideals he could not help but absorb, to which, in pride and humility, he had thereafter dedicated himself. Petri's mother had heard Liszt play in 1880, the "Gretchen" movement of his "Faust" Symphony. Egon described his mother's account:

> He [Liszt] sat down at the piano, after he had taken off his white kid gloves, and deposited them on the piano. He played the second movement, "Gretchen," from his "Faust" Symphony on the piano. She said it was absolutely marvelous, and everybody listened rapturously without saying a word, or even breathing. After he had finished playing he put on his gloves again, bowed very deeply, gave his arm to the Princess of Wittgenstein—and then all the people on both sides of the aisle rose, and bowed very deeply while he was escorting her to the door. It was like a king holding court. It was very impressive and my mother never forgot his playing or the whole atmosphere of the concert.

Egon accompanied his mother on a Blüthner grand piano in the family home. (I will speak more of the Blüthner piano later.) Kathi was, by all accounts, a beautiful young woman and a charming hostess. At one point, Egon recalled, "My mother told me later that Busoni fell in love with her, and went to my father and said, 'I am getting a divorce, and I am going to marry her!'" This was not a jest.

It was Kathi Petri who first suggested to Busoni that he transcribe Bach's organ music. She and Busoni had visited the St. Thomas Church (Bach's own church in Leipzig) one day and heard the organist playing Bach's Prelude and Fugue in D Major. "You ought to arrange that for pianoforte," she said to him. A week later he played it to her. He had not yet written it down. It was the beginning of that style of pianoforte touch and technique which was entirely Busoni's own creation. (See Edward J. Dent's essential biography *Ferruccio Busoni*, Oxford University Press, 1933, p. 82.) Egon added, "My mother told me that he [Busoni] once said to her, when he was twenty years old and a regular guest at my father's house, "If I should find out that I am not as great a composer as Mozart, I shall shoot myself.'"

Of his father's teaching, Egon said, "My father was very strict. A dot and a rest were absolutely sacred. If you didn't keep them— well, he didn't beat me for that, but he did beat me sometimes for being naughty. One time he had an idea to find out if he really hurt me. I found out that he was whipping the floor with the birch and I was screaming just the same!"

Henri Petri had access to two rare violins, a Stradivarius and a Guarnarius. As Egon said, "I used to practice on the Guarnari [*sic*] when my father played his Strad." When Egon was in his teens, he had the use of one or the other for his studying and performing.

Egon advanced rapidly in his violin studies. By age fourteen, he was engaged as violinist in the Dresden Opera Orchestra and sometimes played second violin in his father's string quartet. He was farther ahead in his violin studies than in his keyboard studies. His father expected Egon to become a double-virtuoso: violinist and conductor.

Meanwhile, Egon was busy studying the piano. Of his first keyboard lesson, at age five, given to him "in jest" by Busoni, Egon again stated whimsically, "I think now that was a very cruel birthday present. For a five-year-old, a chocolate would have been much more welcome."

Of his continuing violin studies, Egon said,

When I was sixteen, I played the Bach Chaccone on the violin and the piano. Certain things satisfied me much more on the violin because I could swell and dim in forming the tone and make it so warm. Where, on the piano, the tones could only follow each other and simulate this effect. Still, on the piano, I could make the opening chords so splendid, where on the violin, the drawing of the bow across the strings could go wee, wee, wee.

(Baroque bows, with slacker strings which allowed playing chords on the violin, had not yet been resurrected when Egon was young.) And so it went, round and round, violin . . . piano . . . violin . . .

Early piano instruction from Böhm commenced at age eleven onward. "He probably made me play Czerny exercises and studies, and I wasn't interested in that at all. I remember one Czerny Dexterity Volume (there are two) where it says, 'Knuckles low, fingers high, wrist loose.'" (Here Egon cocked an eyebrow and looked at the ceiling.) "Fortunately, I was always lazy and always got out of practicing when I could. I was always enjoying myself at the piano." Piano lessons with the great Teresa Carreño[5] and Eugene d'Albert were also a

---

[5] Teresa Carreño was a renowned Venezuelan pianist (1853–1917). She gave her first public recital at age eight. Driven out of her country by revolution, her family settled in New York in 1862. She became a student of Louis Gottschalk in the United States and of Anton Rubinstein in Europe. In early adulthood, she lived mostly in Paris, then England. Surprisingly, she became an accomplished opera singer and eventually appeared regularly as singer, pianist, composer, and conductor. Later, in the 1880s, Carreño concentrated more on the piano, touring Germany, even Australia. She was a dynamic, tempestuous personality; for her strength and brilliance, she was

part of his childhood (see chapter 2, "Influences," for more information on d'Albert). Of Teresa Carreño, Egon recalled, "She was considered the greatest and the best." "When I was eleven," he continued, "Carreño was a great friend of my parents. My parents and she exchanged sons—her son Giovani took violin lessons from my mother, and I was sent to her [Carreño] to take piano lessons." Egon said of Carreño that she had "fingers like steel, and trills like electric bells." She demanded lifting the fingers before striking the key, accompanied by low knuckles, immoveable hands and arms, loose wrists, and scales that were to go endlessly up and down the entire keyboard. Slow practice abounded, with fifty or one hundred repetitions of each task. "There seemed but one way to play the piano: hers!"

Reflecting upon all this, Egon said, "I had very bad teachers . . . until I was sent to Carreño, and even Carreño wasn't very good. She said, 'Egon, you must be able to carry a glass of water on your hand'—which contradicts all the rotary business. She played to Breithaupt and he said, 'What are you doing?'—the rotary movement of the arm; she didn't know she was doing it. Her movements were so sparing that she believed that she didn't move anything at all. She never said what it was that made the keys sound loud (the speed of the key, that is) . . . she just did it for me and I tried to imitate it, which is one way of learning to play. . . . Of all the scale playing and immobility, one just had to practice these and find out. I don't think I was very successful. I don't think I'd like her playing very much today, because there wasn't very much music, but a lot of practiced technique—and a very natural technique." Regarding d'Albert, Egon found him a dis-

---

described as "the Valkyrie of the piano." She was one of the first pianists to perform the compositions of Edward MacDowell, who was her pupil. She married four times, the third (1892–1895) to Eugene d'Albert. (She was the first of d'Albert's six wives.) Although she died in New York, her mortal remains were finally interred in Venezuela, where she was greatly revered.

tant personality, at the time wholly engrossed in composing, rather than performing. "All I remember of my lessons with d'Albert is that I would look at the clock, and he would look at his watch." One day, Egon came to his lesson and found the clock had been covered with a cloth. "So, I could no longer see what time it was. But I noticed that d'Albert still regularly glanced at his watch, which I thought was very unfair." Summing up his youthful piano studies, Egon said simply, "I've never been taught properly."

Young Egon enjoyed improvising at the piano, though it was discouraged. "I remember one incident in Dresden," he related. "Father and Mother would go for a walk. . . . Father had said, 'Now Egon, you sit down and practice for an hour, and don't improvise." He continued:

> But when I had seen them gone, I thought, "Well, they won't hear what I am doing," and I began to improvise. We had three maids [servants] at that time, one cook and two maids. They sang in thirds and were used to all these singing lessons and violin lessons. . . . Then suddenly the door opened and one of our maids came in and said, "Egon, you're not practicing, you're improvising. I shall tell your father!" Of course, I never thought they'd know the difference, but they did—they were so musical. They got so much music, we always had our quartet rehearsals in our home."

This incident reflects Egon's early joy in, and propensity for, improvisation, a frequent precursor to composition. In fact, Egon did do some composing, early on. (See the story of his "Nocturne," in chapter 2, "Influences.")

Of Busoni's occasional piano sessions, Egon recounted they were mostly far-ranging illustrated discussions on many subjects: musical, literary, philosophical, polemical. As Egon said, "Once I figured out how many times I played for Busoni during the thirty-eight years I knew him: it was not more than a dozen times." In the end, Egon called Busoni rather a "mentor," and himself a "disciple." For Egon, as for everyone else, Busoni was this charismatic, demonic personage: pianist, composer, conductor, transcriber, visionary.

Looking back, Egon realized that Busoni was, in the end, a mixed blessing. He was too dominant, too influential, too opinionated for an impressionable young man. "He [Busoni] really did me a lot of harm as well as good," Egon said. Although Busoni was generous with knowledge, advice, contacts, time, money (he borrowed money he never intended to give back, and loaned money he never expected to be returned, and like Liszt, he never charged for lessons), Egon later felt that "We were only a kind of mirror in which he reflected himself and admired himself."

Busoni could also be a wayward ideal. "Busoni would take liberties . . . and sometimes he went quite haywire," Egon recalled; other times, "he would play perfectly normally." Busoni once said, "I'm not interested in playing a piece unless I can change it." Egon felt "this reflected the example of Liszt whom Busoni admired above all other pianists, and not only as such, but as composer, innovator, arranger, and gigantic personality generally." At one early point, Egon said, "I wanted to be original like Busoni. It's one of the worst things you can do. Just be the humble servant of the composer." This last statement can stand as a summation of Egon's credo as an artist. As he said sixty years later, "I never wanted to be the first pianist in the world. Of course, there is no such thing."

Even as late as 1939, when Egon performed the monumental five-movement Busoni piano concerto with Frederick Stock and the Chicago Orchestra, his intimate association with Busoni was still uppermost in the public mind. (Egon had performed the Busoni Concerto in England in 1937, and long before, in 1909, with Busoni conducting. See chapter 2 "Influences" and chapter 3 "Teaching" for more on Busoni.)

Through his home years, besides playing the violin for the opera orchestra, second violin for Henri Petri's string quartet, and other chamber performances, Egon also played the piano for his father's chamber music sessions, on the Blüthner grand piano at home, or sometimes elsewhere. "I once played the Kreutzer sonata with my father in a private home in Weisenberg in Breman," he recalled. "I was very young and enthusiastic and we came to the theme in the middle, and I just went to town, and I played it and enjoyed it very much. Suddenly, my father put down his violin and said, 'Please give me a trombone!' I was playing so loud. I was just killing him. So, one learns."

Other early appearances as pianist included Beethoven's "Kreutzer" Sonata in Halle in 1899 and the Brahms D Minor Sonata in Dresden in 1899 with his father, and after Egon left home, Busoni's Sonata Op. 36a in Wiesbaden in 1902, Schumann's Piano Quartet Op. 47 in Zwickau in 1910 (Schumann's birthplace), and Beethoven's "Spring" Sonata Op. 24 in Grossenhain in 1914, the year his father died. Egon was then thirty-three years old.

Throughout his life, Egon admired his father immensely, and treasured these memories. (See the section on Henri Petri in chapter 2, "Influences.") In 1905, Egon married his sweetheart Mitta Schön. The ceremony took place in his parents' home in Dresden. In due time, three children appeared, Jan, Peter, and Ulla, a new Petri family. By 1914, the Petri duo consisted of father and son, Henri and Egon—both fathers.

Later, Egon also played and toured with the great Hungarian violinist Joseph Szigeti, who had acquired the Guarnerius after Henri Petri's death. They first met in Busoni's home in 1912. The two toured the English provinces and gave many sonata recitals in Soviet Russia in the late 1920s. Egon related,

> I played with Szigeti in Russia and one day he had to go out and bow and bow and bow (to acknowledge the fierce, continuing ap-

plause), and he always kept the violin under his arm, and he was tired of keeping it under his arms and he said, "Petri, hold my violin for me. You've been a violinist and you know how to hold one." And I took it and felt so at home, and he came back after the applause had died down, and said, "Petri, did you recognize that violin?" I looked at it, and I said, "Blimey, this is my own Guarnerius— my father's!" I was holding my own little violin.

There is an EMI recording of Szigeti and Petri performing Brahms' D Minor Sonata, Op. 108, recorded in 1937. This is a formidable, revelatory performance. To hear their plasticity of tempo, Petri's fluency and full pedaling, are so revealing. The deliberate regularity of tempi, exquisite phrasing, Szigeti's limited use of vibrato, and the woody, dusky piano sound are likewise very instructive. This performance comes directly out of Brahms' time; Brahms had heard and admired Henri Petri's interpretation of his violin sonatas. Egon was sixteen when Brahms died. Petri summed up his approach to his musical partnership with Szigeti succinctly: "Sonata playing should never be called accompanying."

Because of his father's plans for him regarding conducting, Egon was given instruction on other instruments, especially the horn and organ. Once, when practicing the organ, "which I loved to play," the person hired to pump the bellows suddenly put his head around the corner of the console and pleaded, "Sir, could you please play softer for a while? I'm out of breath here." Egon advanced enough to give a few organ recitals in his teens. "And I loved to make the feet fly," he recalled, especially when playing Bach and César Franck. One recital included the following: Reger Fantasy, the last three chorales of Franck, and a trio sonata of Bach. Egon remembered his organ instructor, Uso Seifert (1852–1912), then a prominent German organist living in Dresden.

One speculates that it influenced Egon's pianism to have inside knowledge of the original instruments called for in certain of Liszt's or Busoni's Bach transcriptions, for example, the violin (Bach's Chaconne) and the pipe organ (Bach's "St. Anne" Prelude and Fugue).

Family Life

Recalling the vibrant cultural life of Dresden, Egon said, "Every day there was an opera, and every day there was a drama or comedy in the playhouse." He attended the orchestral concerts regularly during his teen years. "I was always taken to the concerts, sometimes reluctantly, for I didn't always want to go."

Of family life, Egon related, "My father had the habit of inviting everyone who appeared with the Dresden Symphony to dinner." Guests over the years included Johannes Brahms, Clara Schumann, Anton Rubinstein, Joseph Joachim, Edvard Grieg, Ferruccio Busoni, and Wilhelm Backhaus (whose "pearling scales" had dazzled Egon as a child). Other guests included Gustav Mahler, Peter Tchaikovsky, and Richard Strauss. For most of us, these are historical figures, while to Egon they were family friends.

Egon related that once as a small boy, he invited himself into the upstairs study of his home, where a guest, Gustav Mahler, was sitting at a desk working on a manuscript. Somehow, Egon reached out, upsetting the ink bottle and spilling ink on Mahler's score. Unaccountably, the volatile composer was not upset or angry, but was instead "very sweet, very kind." "It's fine, it's fine, it doesn't matter a bit," said Mahler, trying to soothe the small boy. (The work in question was Mahler's arrangement of Weber's *Die drei Pintos*, later premiered in Leipzig on 20 January 1888. Egon was then seven years old.)

Egon told the story, related by his father, that after an orchestral rehearsal, the elder Petri spoke with Brahms, inviting him to dinner after the upcoming concert. Brahms thought for a moment, then asked, "Is Tchaikovsky coming?" "Oh, no," replied Henri. After another silence, Brahms said, "Then I will come."

The Semper Opera House in Dresden, where Henri Petri served as concertmaster of the opera-orchestra and where, from the age of 14, Egon was a member of the orchestra. The building was completely destroyed in World War II and later reconstructed. (Photo by jvargas on Flckr, shared under a CC BY-SA 2.0 license.)

Young Egon remembered Brahms very well, especially the enormous beard, grand chest, and the permeating odor of tobacco fumes from Brahms' cigars, which, unless completely consumed, were most carefully extinguished and stored in his jacket. Egon remembered that Brahms always had candies or sweets in his pockets for the youngsters. One could even reach into Brahms' pockets to investigate and gather treasures. "It was not easy," said Egon, "for a little boy to sit on Brahms' lap" (because of Brahms' imposing girth).

Of Brahms' beloved Clara, Egon once told us, "I met Clara Schumann when I was five years old." She was absolutely revered by both Egon's parents. Clara Schumann, too, was consulted later regarding Egon's education and future profession.

Egon recalled,

> I remember Richard Strauss came to dinner. I accompanied him back
> to his hotel, and he told me that it took him three-quarters of a year to
> write the G-flat major passage in "Heldenleben." I was very im-
> pressed by that, because I was enormously fond of that piece when I
> first heard it performed. I saw him later when his "Alpen" Symphony
> was performed, and I was very much impressed with it, although I
> don't like it so much now. I was very surprised when he recognized
> me and greeted me in the artists' room after the rehearsal. I was also
> very surprised when he asked all his friends to come to his house and
> play skat, which is a kind of German card game, and have some beer.

Another guest Egon recalled vividly was Joachim, who "wasn't especially hearty. He was a very imposing figure, very tall, with a beautiful hair and beard, a rather formal person. I heard him later on play
with the quartet. Also, much later in Berlin, the Beethoven Concerto."
Joachim disapproved when Egon did not become his scholarship student in Berlin in 1901, Egon deciding instead on a career as a pianist.
Joachim remained resentful the rest of this life. (See footnote 20 for
more on Joachim and Henri Petri.)

Egon also shared memories of Wilhelm Backhaus[6]:

---

[6] Wilhelm Backhaus (1884–1969), eminent German-born Swiss pianist and
pedagogue. He studied in Leipzig with Alois Reckendorf in 1891–1899 and
made his debut there at the age of eight. He studied briefly with Eugene
d'Albert in Frankfurt (1899) and toured Europe. He made his US debut in
1912 as soloist in Beethoven's Fifth Piano Concerto with Walter Damrosch
and the New York Symphony Orchestra. In 1930, he settled in Lugano and
became a Swiss citizen. Following World War II, he resumed his concert
tours. He last appeared in the United States in 1962 (the year of Egon's
death) at the age of seventy-eight. He died while visiting Austria for a concert engagement. According to *Baker's Dictionary*, "He was particularly

One day, little Wilhelm Backhaus came to our home. He had the same shade of hair as Paderewski, only Paderewski's was like a golden mane and his was like straw. Backhaus was eleven years old, and played a concerto with the symphony orchestra. My father asked him to have dinner with us. (I think this was either after the performance or the rehearsal.) Before we sat down at table (it was always playing first, then eating afterwards, which is always a good plan), my father said, "Well, now, you boys make some music together." So I took my violin in hand, and Backhaus sat at the piano, and we played a Mozart sonata together. After we had done that, my father said, "Why don't you play some duets?" So we sat down at the piano and played (I don't remember what). I played the bass. I was thirteen, two years older than Backhaus. . . . I felt very much inferior. I watched him slyly, as it were, out of the corner of my eye. He never watched the keys, scales were like a row of pearls, trills like electric bells, and I said to myself, "Well, I will never be able to do that. . . ." This is where my inferiority complex as a pianist comes from which I have always had from that time. Now at the end of my life, when I heard my last Liszt recording, I said, "Well, after all, other people don't do that very much better than I do." But, I was also surprised when my recordings came out . . . because I always compared it to the ideal I had, and it was never reaching that.

I think a few decades ago, I played as clean scales and as brilliant trills as he did, but at that time it made a very great impression on me.

We met later in life. We met in London and Berlin; the last time I saw him, he played those Beethoven sonatas in San Francisco. His encore was "Soiré de Vienne" [of Schubert-Liszt], and it was really stunning. I have never heard Backhaus play so interestingly and thrillingly. And I really felt a tiny bit of envy there, which I didn't

---

distinguished in his interpretations of the works of Beethoven and Brahms."
He made many recordings.

feel in the Beethoven sonatas at all. "I can do that, too," I said. We all do that. . . . We met and had dinner at Jack's, and his wife was there, and we talked like old friends.

Earlier, in Berlin, his brother at one time became my concert agent, and he said to me (in a very broad Saxon accent), "You know, Mr. Petri, my brother (Wilhelm) has made great progress. He even plays wrong notes now!"

Egon remembered an encounter with Alexander Siloti[7] during his early years:

Once I and Siloti played the Anton Rubinstein Violin Sonata [with Egon playing the violin part]. I remember the Scherzo in A-minor, and it went in thirds. I remember him saying to me, "Of course nobody plays these thirds. I only play the upper part, you see." I thought that very cowardly for a famous pianist.

He (Siloti) had the idea that Liszt was always standing as a ghost directing his playing and telling him exactly what to do. He really believed that! He was a kind of spiritualist. I heard him play several times, and I thought him very sloppy.

Egon recalled an incident with Carl Reinecke (1824–1910), as well:

Old Reinecke and the Schumann Quintet: I once played the Schumann Quintet with my father in Halle (where Reinecke was the professor of piano). Now, I played the second violin part, and old

---

[7] Alexander Siloti (1863–1945) was a famed pupil of Nicholai Rubinstein, Tchaikovsky, and Liszt. He was Gold Medal Winner at the Moscow Conservatory, becoming a highly successful Russian concert pianist, conductor, and teacher. Rachmaninoff was one of his pupils (his first cousin). Siloti left Russia in 1919, and settled in New York in 1922. He was on the faculty of the Juilliard School of Music from 1925 to 1942. He later published a book of his reminiscences of Liszt (with whom he had studied until Liszt's death in 1886).

Reinecke played the piano part and I remember still the urgent desire I had to push this old man away from the piano, put down my violin, and play the piano. "I can do this much better than you," I thought.

One notes how cruel youth can be. In fact, in his prime, Carl Reinecke was a towering piano virtuoso. Early on, he had crucial contact with Mendelssohn and Schumann, and later taught at the Leipzig Conservatory. He made many highly successful concert tours in Europe: the Netherlands, Scandinavia, Switzerland, Germany, and England. He was a conductor of the Gewandhaus Concerts in Leipzig from 1860–1898! A prolific composer, he wrote four technically taxing piano concertos, three symphonies, several operas, a violin concerto, a cello concerto, three sonatas for two pianos, and considerable chamber music. As well, he wrote books, one on the Beethoven piano sonatas.

There is a recording of Michael Ponti performing Reinecke's Second Piano Concerto with spectacular virtuosity. Therein is one seeming impossibility heaped upon another. And there are three more such concertos! Sadly, now, Reinecke's compositions seem strangely derivative, temporal. Such is Fate!

All this did not count to young Egon, who was so firmly fixed upon the fecund present, and the radiant future.

Egon also spoke of meeting Rainer Maria Rilke (1875–1926):

Then, the next year I went to Berlin. I was twenty-one and I began to practice! (the piano). I went to Worpswede, near Bremen. I met Heinrich Vogler there. He was a very famous book illustrator. At his house was Maria Rilke—at the same time I was there. I am mentioned in his diaries. There is a letter existing which I saw: he says to his wife, "There is a young man here called Petri who plays Bach beautifully." She was a sculptress, and a pupil of Rodin. She was very strong and big, like a country horse, and he [Rilke]was a tiny man, narrow-chested, with a tiny voice, and a very thin little beard. Once, in Bremen we went to a party, and he read his poems in a tiny wee voice, and I thought "Now this woman must surely dominate

Young Egon Petri, from *The Piano Library: Egon Petri,* a CD set released by S.A.I.E. in 1996, featuring recordings from the period 1929–1938.

him." It was exactly the other way 'round. She was his obedient slave. And he didn't look like this. Vogler had a guest book and Rilke put a little poem each day in his guest book as a kind of contribution.

In fact, Rilke's wife, Clara Westhoff, was not a pupil of Rodin, though she dearly wished to be. Rilke's tangled relationship with Rodin, as secretary and biographer, is freshly illuminated in a recent book, *You Must Change Your Life: Rainer Maria Rilke and Rodin* by Rachel Corbett (Norton 2016). In Petri's twenty-first year, Rilke was just twenty-seven years old, still ten years from beginning the *Duino Elegies*, and twenty years from penning the *Sonnets to Orpheus* in that great outburst. Rilke's story is one of amazing growth, development—change—until the clarification of his final insight into that "World-inner space." Obviously, young Egon, here, saw Rilke still in transition, still in a formative phase.

Schooling

Egon's education included the Burgher School, a cadet military school (not a surprising choice during that era), and sessions with tutors. These included Herman Kretzschmar (composition, Leipzig Conservatory), Richard Buchmayer (piano, Dresden Conservatory), and Felix Draeseke (theory, Dresden Conservatory). Although they surely contributed to Egon's education, he said little of them to me. He mentioned only Draeseke: "He was a very, very queer fellow and always analyzed Beethoven's symphonies for me and played a bit, and also played his own compositions. I don't think I learned very much. I brought him my own compositions, and he didn't quite know what to do with me."

An aspect of his education that Egon recalled with more detail and enthusiasm was his early thespian love of declaiming, especially Goethe and Schiller. Egon never lost his vibrant baritone voice with its elegant British English (he had learned his English early in Dresden from tutors among the active English colony there). "In our literature classes, we were given plays by Goethe and Schiller, or Shakespeare in German translation, and we had to read the different parts. I loved being Egmont in Goethe. I read it with the greatest delight, and I was very good at that."

Besides his fondness for declaiming, he recalled, "I sang in the choir in school. I had perfect pitch and was one of the mainstays of the chorus. In choir, we sang chorales of Bach, other German chorales, masses by Hasse, and various classics of Mozart and Haydn. . . . I had no difficulty in singing. I *loved* singing!"

Throughout his life, Egon would speak English, French, German, Italian, Polish, or Russian at any time, taking an innocent delight in his favorite form of wit—puns. He was once upset over his limited knowledge of Dutch. After each of two command performances for

Queen Wilhelmina of the Netherlands, she and Egon had to converse in German, which he greatly regretted, since his heritage (and his passport) proclaimed him to be Dutch.

Egon remembered the rector of the Burgher school:

> Fortunately, the rector of the school was an amateur violinist, and sometimes he would ask me to come up to his apartment, which was at the "School of the Cross," where Wagner went. He would say, "Egon, would you come up and play a violin sonata by Mozart or Beethoven with me?" Then he would give me lunch. All my school fellows were very envious, and thought, "What is he, that he is on such good terms with the rector." But, of course, he knew my father, and admired him, and knew that I played very well, and he needed somebody to accompany him."

Egon's parents noticed that he was not very interested in school. "We had about thirty members in our class," he recalled. "We were seated according to scholastic standing. To the left was the primus, then came secundo, and then came I. My mother said to me, 'Now Egon, if you made a little effort, couldn't you be the first one in class?' I said, 'You know, mother, you mustn't always want to be the first one. One must leave something to other people, too!"

Finally, Egon became critically bored with the cadet school. He begged his father for private tutoring in order to be able to finish two years in one. His father relented, tutors were engaged, and Egon's schooling ended satisfactorily a year early.

Piano versus Violin: A Difficult Decision

At age twenty, Egon gave up the violin, to his father's deep regret. Henri Petri asked Joseph Joachim and Ignace Paderewski to advise him regarding Egon's future career. Recalling these discussions, Egon said, "So, I was very glad Paderewski did not say I should not become a pianist, and that Joachim did say I *should* be a violinist. Paderewski did not hear me play the violin, but it is quite enough for me that he encouraged me to become a pianist. That was really the turning point in my life. I had great admiration for him." As already stated, Joachim wished Egon to become his scholarship pupil in Berlin.

Henri Petri also asked the advice of Brahms (in the last year of the composer's life, 1897). Brahms recommended that Egon finish school before concertizing. That way, Brahms said, if music should ever fail Egon, he would have other resources. By letter, Clara Schumann held the opposite opinion, advising the Petris to send their gifted son to the Conservatory at once! Egon was grateful for Brahms' advice, for he wished to complete his schooling.

Curiously, at eighteen years of age, everyone said Egon looked just like Brahms, and they all called him "Johannes." Recalling this odd resemblance, he remarked, "How strange!" Of his farewell to violin studies, Egon said, "I wept tears because I loved my violin."

Looking closely at his home life, Egon recalled, "When I was twenty in Busoni's master class in Weimar . . . it was the first time I had left home. And I was glad. [At home] I was always asked, 'Have you practiced?' Have you done your schoolwork?' 'Have you practiced the piano?'—And if I came home from school and talked to a friend and lingered a little bit for a walk—why, my mother would stand at the door and my father would send for the police to search for me. I couldn't be a quarter of an hour late without getting into trouble."

As Egon recalled, "When I played [performed] the violin for the last time, I played Busoni's Second Sonata. I played the violin, and Busoni played the piano, and he said, 'I have never heard it played better.'"

Egon mused over his difficulty in choosing between the violin and the piano:

As my father was a violinist, I didn't want to be the second violin in the family, even though I was confused with him [my father] sometimes. People would stand in the Guest Artist room and say, "Are you Professor Petri with whom my friend studied, or are you his son, the pianist?" This happened very often.

Other reasons why I preferred the piano to the violin: first the extent (treble and bass), and then the melodious harmonic expression. Sometimes in the last years when I would play a melody on the piano, I would think, "If I only had a violin that could vibrate and join things and play legato." But I thought also the literature is so much more extensive on the piano. Beethoven wrote one violin concerto, Brahms wrote only one, etc. . . . And then there's Chopin! I thought eventually I wanted to become a conductor.

As for conducting, it is much more important to play the piano. I could play the scores, and accompany the singers. So, it was a practical thing. I can't say I ever loved the piano as much as I loved the violin. But I have been much happier with the piano. You see, I would have had to play in a quartet, and hate my other three colleagues (which my father, too, hated . . . and they hated him). All quartet members I know hate each other. The Budapest Quartet—they worked it out: they never speak to each other. Another thing, I would have had to be in an orchestra, but for the grace of God!

These remarks provide primary clues to Egon's artistry. Lifelong, he approached scores as a conductor, perceiving each composition as a whole, with its particular architecture, before considering its individual elements, and their emotional/psychological expression.

Also, Egon's feeling for melody (which he called "melodiousness") emanated more from the violin than the piano. His concept of colors, too, largely came from the violin—and the orchestra—both of which were so familiar to him. When Egon played, all voices were living lines, as in a string quartet or orchestra, and a pianistic tutti would have the feel of an orchestral tutti, in its impact and fulsomeness. In

Baker's Dictionary of Music and Musicians, Nicholas Slonimsky referred to "Petri's own conception of piano playing as the fullest representation, by a single instrument, of the sonorities of an orchestra."

Egon said,

> A pianist, I always say, is an irresponsible being—he can play twice as fast or twice as loud because nobody suffers from it except the people who know something about music—there are very few in an audience. But in a quartet or in an opera, you can't play it as you like, so I'm always for starting with a stringed instrument.

> If my own child had to learn music, . . . he/she should first study the violin for finding the pitch, then take to the piano—not the other way. Wind instruments and singing are much easier to phrase—there is a natural end to the bow and to the breath, not on the piano. You can play a staccato or legato on the piano for one hour without interrupting, but you can't do this on other instruments, and you don't learn to phrase on the piano.

These ruminations certainly reflect Egon's own experiences in his early training.

Marriage and First Teaching Position

Later, the violin and Beethoven had their influence once again. In 1905, Egon, now twenty-four and desperate to obtain a teaching post so that he could marry his beloved Mitta Schön (despite total opposition from Mitta's father), nearly took a position at the Cincinnati Conservatory. But, Busoni, not wanting Egon so far away ("Busoni used me in many ways to work for him"), had heard of a position opening up in Manchester, England, at the Royal College of Music (where Backhaus was leaving). Its director, Adolph Brodsky,[8] was then vaca-

---

[8] Adolph Brodsky (1851–1929), famous Russian violin virtuoso. Debut at age nine in Odessa. A pupil of Hellmesberger in Vienna. Later, professor in

tioning in Marianbad, Austria. Busoni said, "Send him a telegram." Egon did, and the next day received a reply from Brodsky to come see him. Now, here was a crisis—Egon had no money for the trip! He recalled, "Just at the same time I got an offer to make pianola records for a firm in Leipzig—they offered me 500 marks for so many recordings. Here was the finger of fate again!"

With characteristic modesty, Egon continued:

> I made these recordings which weren't very good. I took the marks and visited Brodsky in Marianbad. . . . Now Brodsky said, "Petri, do you know the Kreutzer Sonata?" "Of course, I've played it with my father." Brodsky said, "I have no music here," and I said, "I have no music," and he said, 'Well, just let's play it together." I said, "fine.". . . I knew it from memory. So, we played it together and he was convinced I could do something. And he made me play other things and was very, very satisfied. He went back to Manchester . . . and proposed my name. On the first of October, I got a telegram, "You are appointed."

Moscow Conservatory. In 1881 made a European tour. With Brahms' deep gratitude, Brodsky championed Brahms' Violin Concerto soon after its writing, in 1879. Also, in 1881 (Egon's birth year), Brodsky gave the world premier of Tchaikovsky's Violin Concerto in Vienna. Taught at Leipzig Conservatory, 1883–1891. In 1891–1894, served as concertmaster of the New York Philharmonic. In 1895, went to Manchester as concertmaster of Halle orchestra. Principal of Royal College in 1896. Another gifted virtuoso who lived an eventful but endlessly peripatetic life. Later (while in Manchester, England), Brodsky was the main teacher of Naoum Blinder, for many years concertmaster of the San Francisco Symphony (from 1932 onward). Blinder, in turn, was the principal teacher of Isaac Stern (1920–2001). As a grand-pupil of Brodsky, Stern remained a major force in violin performance and teaching for most of the twentieth century.

Now Egon could marry Mitta, who, in an extremely brave move for that time, defied her father, left her home, and joined Egon in Dresden, where they were married in the Petri home. Thereafter, they left for Manchester, where they remained from 1905 to 1911. Here, then, was the influence of the violin and Beethoven at life's crossroads!

Egon later gave chamber recitals with Brodsky, a truly worthy partner. For example, in 1912, in Manchester, their program was as follows: Spohr Adagio from Concerto Op. 55 (arr.), Beethoven Sonata in G, Op. 30, no. 3, Brahms Sonata in G, Op. 78, and Schubert Rondeau brilliante Op. 70.

Interlude: Piano Wars and Dream Pianos

Now, a further word about Egon Petri's pianos, his attitudes toward pianos, as well as the larger picture of the pianos of those times, starting with the Petri family's Blüthner piano. In Vienna, Mahler had kept a Blüthner grand in his studio. In Russia, Rachmaninoff, too, kept a Blüthner grand on his estate. Indeed, the Blüthner must have been a premier chamber piano to be so widely favored, by the Petris, Rachmaninoff, and Mahler.[9]

Lately (2015), Mrs. K. and I, while visiting the National Museum of American History in Washington, D.C., came upon Rach-

---

[9] Julius Blüthner (1824–1910), piano builder, founded his firm in 1853 in Leipzig. The firm eventually produced three thousand pianos yearly. The Blüthner pianos were awarded many medals. As Rachmaninoff wrote, "On leaving Russia, I took with me two things: one, my wife; two, my Blüthner piano." Mahler's Blüthner grand, built in 1902, is now housed in the Kunsthistorisches Museum in Vienna. Blüthner's factory near Leipzig was destroyed during an air raid in 1943. The Russian occupying forces allowed the family to rebuild after World War II. The Blüthner firm was put under state control in 1972; after 1989, the family bought back the company. It is now managed by Mr. Blüthner-Haessler and his two sons.

maninoff's Blüthner grand, now housed there. We played on it for a few moments—a sweet, velvety sound, luminous treble and burnished bass, with a "halo" of after-sounds, partially due to the extra layer of treble strings which are not struck but instead vibrate sympathetically (it is called an "Alquotflügel").

In his first concertizing, Egon favored the Bechstein pianos. He admired the Hamburg Steinways, too, but that firm demanded an exclusive contract, "and I was not willing to give up my Bechsteins completely."[10] It was later that Egon made an arrangement to use the

---

[10] Carl William Friedrich Bechstein (1826–1900), piano builder, founded his firm in 1853 (the same year as the Blüthner firm!) in Berlin. Eventually, branches were established in France, Russia, and England. A grandson held the firm until 1931. It is now an independent firm. *Baker's Dictionary* (1984) says, "Possesses a particularly harmonious tone, capable of producing a mellifluous cantilena; for many years it was the favorite instrument of pianists of the romantic school." Unfortunately, a Carl Bechstein, along with other German industrialists such as I.G. Farben, Thyssen, and Krupp, helped bankroll the rise of Hitler in 1930–1933, which eventually led to the deaths of so many millions, and the dislocation of many more millions, including Petri, Bruno Walter, Szigeti, Toscanini, Klemperer, Bartok, etc., and the total destruction of Germany in 1945. Hitler first met many of these industrialists in the mansion of Carl and Helene Bechstein in Berlin. The Bechstein firm was confiscated during the denazification of Germany at war's end. In 1993, it had to be rescued from bankruptcy by the city of Berlin. Since then, the firm has risen again, their pianos regaining stature. By 2002, the firm was again building some three thousand new Bechsteins a year. Recent Bechsteins we have heard in recordings (in 2017) are not nearly as mellow as the earlier models. Considerable lacquering has been applied to the hammers, and seemingly not only for American audiences. Yet, only a few years ago, I performed a recital in Bend, Oregon, on a new Bechstein grand, with a lustrous, mellow sound, and a friendly action, so different from these.

European Hamburg Steinway and American Steinway exclusively. This also meant passing up not only the Bechstein and Blüthner pianos, but also the riches of the Bösendorfer and Ehrbar (Brahms' favorite) in Vienna, and the Ibach in Germany. How ironic to have two famous piano firms in Vienna, one named Bösendorfer ("bad citizen") and the other, Ehrbar ("honorable citizen"). Of course, Brahms chose the latter.

Besides Egon Petri, Schnabel, Busoni, and Dinu Lipatti (1917–1950) used the Bechstein. (However, in Paris, Busoni discovered an Erard that he treasured. He used Hamburg Steinway pianos in Germany, also.) In fact, Schnabel used the Bechstein for his epochal recording of all the Beethoven piano sonatas, 1932–1935, recordings still in print. As Schnabel said, "Bechstein was, in Germany, what Steinway is in the States, and Bösendorfer in Vienna." Debussy remarked that "piano music should only be written for Bechsteins." (Ravel and Wagner, contrarily, preferred the French Erard. Mrs. K. and I played on Ravel's Erard grand in his home in Montfort, France, which is now a museum. How different it was from the Bechstein of Egon and Debussy, with its drier, leaner, more harp-like sonorities!) The piano firms contended fiercely for exclusive contracts with the prominent pianists of the day. Early on, at the instigation of Busoni, Egon played a concert on the Ibach piano. (Ibach was trying to get Busoni to commit to their pianos.) As Egon said, "I played their piano [Ibach] once in Berlin, and Steinway was so mad at me for playing on that piano that they threatened to get rid of me. So, it really did me a disservice." The piano wars!

Egon played many times in Wigmore Hall, London, also performing historic concerts there with Busoni in 1921 and 1922 (including the two-piano version of Busoni's Fantasia contrappuntistica). Egon told us that Wigmore Hall was formerly named Bechstein Hall and that it was renamed during World War I, when everything German became anathema to the English. (Busoni and Petri appeared to-

gether as well in Berlin and Paris.) Bechsteins and Hamburg Steinways were always available.

Egon was using the Hamburg Steinway by the time he performed the five Beethoven concertos in Amsterdam with the Concertgebouw Orchestra under Willem Mengelberg, and first played the
Beethoven sonata cycle in England in 1908 (at age twenty-six or
twenty-seven). When he performed the thirty-two sonatas for the last
time in San Francisco, in 1959 (at age seventy-eight), he was using
the American Steinway.[11]

Egon toured America for the first time in 1932, playing from
coast to coast on American Steinway pianos. Well before this, he had
formed an agreement with Hamburg Steinway in 1905 in England.
From then on he was given three Steinway grands: one for home use,
one for his studio, and one for the concert hall. Every four years,
Steinway replaced the home piano, assuming it had undergone
enough hard usage. As Egon said, "Those were the good times. This
sounds like the Arabian Nights now." (Mrs. K. and I had our lessons
with Egon on these pianos.)

Late in his life, upon moving to different quarters in California,
Egon decided to return his home Steinway to the Steinway headquarters in New York City. Upon being notified, Steinway had no record
of Egon having one of their instruments. No contract had ever been
signed!

---

[11] Mrs. K. and I also appeared several times in Wigmore Hall (solo and
duo), as well as in the Concertgebouw. For our duo work in each of these
halls, we used a Hamburg Steinway and a beauteous Bechstein piano, essentially compatible instruments, with the Bechstein a little less bright, but
mellifluous, sonorous. Let us say, too, that the Hamburg Steinways were,
like the Bechsteins, always kept in exemplary condition, with their bell-like
sound and fleet Renner actions. We felt keenly that in their sound—and indeed, by their very existence—they were echoes of European history!

Once, in the late 1950s, a group of pianists were bemoaning the derelict concert-piano situation in the United States—instruments not properly tuned, inadequately voiced, uneven touch, and Teflon actions (making them unduly stiff), etc. We finally asked Egon, "How do you feel about all this?" He thought for a moment, and replied, "Listen, my Dear Children, there is a piano on the stage. When the time comes, you go out and you play on that piano, and do the very best you can."

I recall Sviatoslav Richter playing a splendid all-Beethoven sonata program on an American Steinway in San Francisco during his first American tour in 1960. After the concert, Egon, Mrs. K., and I went backstage to congratulate Richter, who was immensely moved to meet Egon again after so many years. Richter gave Egon a Russian bear hug and kept praising him, saying he had never forgotten Egon's tours in Russia, that he had heard Egon often, had followed him from concert to concert, and that Egon's playing had influenced him so much as a young man.[12]

---

[12] Egon toured Russia first in 1914. Later, he was the first Western artist to enter the Soviet Union after the revolution. Altogether he played more than three hundred recitals in Russia. He once played thirty-five concerts in forty-one days. He seldom repeated programs on tour, since he knew that a portion of his audience followed him from concert to concert (as Richter did). He once had to give thirty-three encores. His programs were usually huge, and took in vast stores of repertoire. Often there were lengthy intermissions, with many "toasts" of vodka. Egon was young, gifted, brave, and luckily, very healthy. As he said, "I was never tired, although I had to work very, very hard."

"The only places where I never had a deficit was in Poland and Russia," Egon recounted. "When they announced Egon Petri in Russia, "3 concerts by E. P."—without a program—police would be there because people were breaking windows, wanting to buy tickets and everything was sold out. The same thing in Poland." Once, in Russia, after a concert, a joyous crowd out in the street was heaving Egon in the air in front of his hotel. His

Curiously, in Monsaignon's *Richter, Notebooks and Conversations*, it states that Richter could never select a piano for a concert (p. 108). The choice terrified him! He said he had played some of his very best concerts on the worst of pianos. Richter felt that a stage and a piano formed a kind of single destiny for an artist, and that one can do no more than accept one's destiny.

Certainly, a wonderful destiny was possible with the magnificent American Steinway concert grand CD-65 in Boston. It was a dream-piano, splendid in every way. With its fulsome, clarion bell-like tones, an exquisitely responsive action, a sensitive and adaptive soft pedal, and a plangent, lustrous bass, everyone who performed in Boston was anxious to rent it, including Egon Petri, Byron Janis, Cliburn, Richter, and Artur Rubinstein (although he usually brought his Hamburg Steinway from Paris). In fact, both Rubinstein and Richter used it for recordings, Richter for his epochal performance of Brahms' Second Concerto, with Leinsdorf conducting. Richter held a violently negative opinion of his recording of the Second Concerto of Brahms with Leinsdorf, in which he had used the CD65, as recounted in Monsaignon's book (cited earlier).[13] So, in this case, Richter had a

---

wife, anxiously awaiting her husband, was at that very moment looking out the window of the hotel room. Imagine her astonishment when her husband's face kept appearing and reappearing before her! During this time, there developed an innocent kind of "piano war" between the Schnabelists of Leningrad and the Petrites of Moscow. Petri related he was once on a train in Russia with Trotsky. Later, Egon heard there had been a bomb plot on that train.

[13] I, too used the CD-65 for my Boston debut in Jordan Hall (Bach-Busoni, Beethoven, Scriabin, Chopin, and the Barber Sonata—a quite Petri-like program, in retrospect). As well, Mrs. K. and I used it for our four-hand debut there. CD-65 was an unforgettable, enchanting, ideal partner, a dream come true.

kind of ideal piano upon which to perform (was it ideal for him?) and still he felt cheated of an ideal performance.

As for me, I think one's dream piano can offer one a rarer, finer destiny, corroborated by almost all the giant musicians of the recent past who have clung to their single, most favorite instrument: Debussy, Ravel, Schnabel, Gieseking, Rubinstein, Horowitz, Michelangeli, etc. Garrick Ohlsson travels with a Bösendorfer, Martha Argerich and Angela Hewitt extol the virtues of the Italian Fazioli (since 1981). (The Juilliard School has purchased several Fazioli grands, which are truly exemplary in their very own way.) In 2015, Daniel Barenboim began collaborating on the invention of a new piano (reportedly, a fresh, eclectic combination of attributes of earlier and recent pianos)—so we will see what becomes of it. (Bösendorfer was acquired by Yamaha in 2008.) It is known, too, that Glen Gould, early, had the hammer stems of his instrument shortened, in order to affect a dryer, more somber sound reminiscent of a harpsichord.

For his 2017 Beethoven cycle recordings, Andras Schiff reportedly chose a Grand Bösendorfer piano for the late sonatas and a Hamburg Steinway for all the others. Meanwhile, 2017 also saw the reprinting in CD form of Walter Gieseking's complete Debussy piano works (Warner Classics). I was once told by a reputable source that Gieseking recorded solely on a grand that, until discovered by Gieseking, had been sitting neglected in a warehouse, deliberately avoided by everyone else. Is this true, or is it a myth? Was it a Bechstein? Or? What is true is that this particular piano used in Gieseking's recordings of Debussy and Ravel, apparently the ideal in-

---

This magnificent CD-65 was crushed a few years later, caught halfway out of a moving elevator. For us all, it was like losing a Stradivarius! Alas, the Petri/Szigeti Guarnerius was similarly annihilated, crushed by a wardrobe case upset by a dockworker somewhere in Japan.

strument for Gieseking, has sound qualities unlike any other, an incomparable, singular meeting of instrument and spirit.

And Egon? His attitude was ultimately pragmatic. Once, after a technician apologized for the condition of the piano, Petri replied, "Listen, there is no such thing as a perfect piano. You just sit down and play it."

To sum up, in Egon's case, the sound on his early recordings is unique to himself, an adaptation of the early Bechstein sound. Later recordings have his earlier American Steinway imprint, while his Basel recordings intimate the earlier Hamburg Steinway sound. Needless to say, the difference between the first and the rest is not small. Perhaps, in the 21st century, a new era will evolve, where each artist will have his/her individual sound, as it was in the late 19th and early 20th centuries.

Interlude: Early Conductors

Egon held vivid memories of various conductors with whom he had performed. "My great friend, Bruno Walter," or "my good friend, Dimitri Mitropoulos" would appear in many of his reminiscences. At least three figured significantly in his early career: Willem Mengleberg (1871–1951), Sir Henry Wood (1869–1944), and Hans Richter (1843–1916).[14] Here is how he spoke of them, candidly, freely, a momentous lifetime later:

---

[14] To name more notable conductors with whom Egon performed: Sir John Barbirolli, Sir Adrian Bolt, Eric Kleiber, Otto Klemperer, Serge Koussevitsky, Dimitri Mitropoulos, Bernardino Molinari, Frederick Stock, Bruno Walter, and Artur Rodzinski (who always carried a loaded revolver in his back pocket whenever he conducted).

Willem Mengelberg[15]—the very famous conductor under whom I
played very often in the Amsterdam Concertgebouw. [Mengelberg,
we note, was only ten years older than Egon.] He was a very disa-
greeable man, but rather a good musician. I remember two things
about him: one was I played the Saint-Saëns Concerto No. 5 where
there is a canon in the second movement, and then the orchestra
comes in. We played this, rehearsing on two pianos. Mengelberg
was very angry, "Petri, you are a bar behind." He didn't know it was
a canon. He simply didn't know the concerto. Another time, which I
thought was very tactless, I played all five Beethoven Concertos in
Amsterdam with him. When I played the Emperor, there was an up-
right in the artists' room, and before we went out to play, he sat
down and said, "I used to play this concerto" and he was playing
through the beginning and being very proud of himself. It really isn't
a good idea of a conductor, when a young artist is about to go on in
public, to sit down and discourage one (of course, he didn't really)—
he could be a very rude and objectionable man.

I've heard him talk to the different orchestras, and was always ex-
plaining—he should simply have conducted.

---

[15] Willem Mengelberg (1871–1951) was born in Utrecht, Holland. He became music director at Lucerne in 1891, then head of the famous Concertgebouw Orchestra in Amsterdam for fifty years and renowned throughout
Europe. Because he sided with the Nazis during World War II, he was
banned from professional activities in Holland after the country's liberation.
He lived in exile in Switzerland until his final year. *Baker's Dictionary*
says, "Mengelberg was one of the finest representatives of the Romantic
tradition in symphonic conducting. His interpretations extracted the full
emotional power from the music, and yet he never transgressed the limits
imposed by the structural forms of classical music. His renditions of Beethoven's symphonies were inspiring." Mengelberg was a great admirer of
Mahler and champion of Max Reger, Claude Debussy, and Richard Strauss
(who dedicated the score of *Ein Heldenleben* to him).

He became a Quisling during the German occupation and people simply despised him. Once, during the Occupation, he was going to conduct the Concertgebouw Orchestra, and when he raised his baton, the whole orchestra put down their instruments and were absolutely silent. It was a terrible moment for him, but he deserved it. (This happened to Cortot once. My sister heard him say "heil Hitler" once in Dresden. He had no business to say that. She saw him say it of his own free will.[16]

In contrast, Egon said of Sir Henry Wood[17]:

I liked him very much from the beginning. I think I first played the "Malediction" [of Liszt], a very rare piece to hear or find. It is only

---

[16] All we know of Egon's sister is that she was killed in an air raid in Hanover during World War II. We know also that one of his sons became an officer in the British Army.

[17] Sir Henry Wood (1869–1944), eminent English conductor, learned the piano from his mother, participated in many family musicales from the age of six. He was precocious on the organ as well. By age ten, he was deputy organist, giving organ recitals at age fourteen and sixteen. In 1886, he entered the Royal Academy of Music, winning four medals. He composed songs, cantatas, and light operas. He conducted for an opera company, becoming assistant conductor of the Savoy Theatre in 1890. In 1895 (at age twenty-six), he founded his famous "Promenade Concerts" in Queen's Hall (in which Petri regularly participated). Sir Henry founded the Nottingham Orchestra in 1899, and was subsequently conductor of the Wolverhampton, Sheffield, and Norwich festivals. In 1904, he conducted in New York. Knighted in 1911, he was also offered the conductorship of the Boston Symphony, but he declined. He conducted in California in 1925. He married Olga Urusova, a Russian noblewoman, and adopted a Russian pseudonym for his compositions and arrangements. Sir Henry performed Russian music frequently in his concerts. Olga died in 1909; he remarried in 1911 to Murial Greatorex. He conducted the "Promenade Concerts" almost to the end of his life.

for string orchestra. It was in Queen's Hall, and he stopped the orchestra and said, "That is the way Liszt should be played." That was a great compliment to me.

My agent, Robinson, said, "He [Wood] would be the best conductor for you, and he isn't expensive"—He was a beginning conductor with the London Philharmonic. He became later Sir Henry, and became the director of the "Promenade concerts," which he founded.

He invented one thing which was wonderful. He had a man in the artists' room turn a handle [on a machine] to an A, and each member of the orchestra had to come through the artists' room and tune according to that A. They (the orchestra) never tuned up on the stage. Henry Wood would say, "Well, this is all right," "this is a little high," or "this is a little low." I think that was the best idea I have ever seen. He wrote a very interesting book about conducting. Have you read it?"

Of Hans Richter,[18] Egon had an especially vivid array of memories.

---

[18] Hans Richter (1843–1916) was known as an "eminent German conductor," although he was born in Raab, Hungary. He studied theory, violin, and French horn at the Vienna conservatory. From 1862 to 1866, he was employed as a horn player at the Kärthnertor Theatre in Vienna. The turning point in his career was his contact with Wagner in Triebschen (Wagner's house on Lake Lucerne), where he was entrusted to make a fair copy of the score of *Die Meistersinger*. In December of 1870, Richter performed the trumpet part of the first performance of the *Siegried Idyll* in Triebschen, at the foot of the stairs leading to the upper floor and Cosima's chamber, where baby Siegfried had just been born. (Mrs. K. and I had the rare experience of standing at the foot of this stairway, while a recording of the *Idyll* sounded on the speaker system.) Richter subsequently held conducting posts in Munich and Budapest, advancing to premier conductor of the Vienna Philharmonic in the periods 1875–1882 and 1883–1897. He conducted the entire *Ring* cycle at the Bayreuth Festival in 1876, and he conducted Wagner festivals in London beginning in 1879, as well as "Richter" con-

I played several times with Richter. He was very, very old-fashioned. He loved to conduct Brahms and Wagner. He played everything too slowly I think.

He was very large and very heavy. I told you that he never turned his face to the pianist? You see, he always turned his broad back to me, and he was bald, and you always had the idea of the moon rising behind the hill. Of course, I can talk about bald people because I am bald myself. It was absolutely impossible to give him a nod or a cue. He just *conducted*."

"Was there much freedom in his interpretations?" I asked. "No," Egon responded. "*Breit und wichtig*, is the *Meistersinger* Prelude marking, that means 'Broad and ponderous.' He did not like hurried tempi. He was always too slow and heavy and ponderous. But for certain things like Brahms it is very good."

He continued,

Richter was a very very slow individual. He was not a German; Austrians are generally not like that, but his personality was very slow and heavy. He certainly seemed more German than Austrian—or Bavarian. He asked me to come to his house and drink a bottle of red wine with him—he was very nice to me—but very ponderous, and he used to say, 'My garden is not very big, but it's very high.' That was the wittiest remark he ever made. He always wore a flannel jacket. But he loved beer and wine and loved to talk about himself and Wagner, but for him I had the greatest respect because he was an historic figure already. Everyone admired him like a hero. It's only now that I look back and see him in his own perspective. He didn't

---

certs annually until 1897. Richter conducted the Halle Orchestra in Manchester in 1897, as well as festivals in Birmingham and Covent Garden in London. "His technique was flawless," *Baker's* states. Besides Wagner's music Richter gave many performances of the symphonies of Brahms and Elgar.

really deserve the great name, I think. He didn't talk much about music—just heavy-handed jokes, and have-some-more-wine, and it was all very prosaic. But I was a young man and shy and too much in awe of him and his authority. Brodsky, too—I was always afraid of him, more or less.

However, Egon did express admiration for Richter's musicianship when he recalled, "Richter was one of those who, during a rehearsal, could just take the clarinet away from a man and say, after wiping it, 'Well, I want you to do it this way.' So, he could take a bassoon, a horn, and so on." He continued,

In fact, my father was influenced by Richter. My father had heard from Hans Richter that if you wanted to become a conductor, which I always wanted to do, it was a good thing if you could play all the instruments of the orchestra yourself. So I studied the organ and French horn. So it was that I should have learned the clarinet, oboe, etc., but I gave up at that time because I was too busy with school and other things.

Richter was once conducting the *Meistersinger* Prelude in a rehearsal, and there was a doctor who was a very great music lover, but no performer. Richter said to him, "My dear Doctor, I would like to test the balance and I want to go around the Free Trade Hall, upstairs, and downstairs, at the back. It is very hard to tell the balance when the hall is empty. You can't wait until the concert and then walk about, you see. Would you conduct the orchestra for me while I listen?" So, the doctor was very pleased and conducted, and the orchestra did beautifully. It could have played without him quite easily. When Richter came back he said, "Well, thank you, my friend, it is perfectly all right." The doctor said to Dr. Richter, "You know, Doctor, conducting is quite easy. I thought it was much more difficult." And Richter whispered, "I know, but don't tell anybody!"

Now, when I came, Richter was leaving Manchester forever, and gave a farewell concert, and I was leaving Manchester, and I never taught there again. In the last farewell concert, I played the César Franck Variations symphoniques. Just as the bell rang after the intermission (I was with Richter in the artists' room, the Green room), and we were to go out, Richter said to me, "Petri, would you like to conduct?" I didn't know what he meant or why he brought up the question. I said, "Well, I always wanted to be a conductor, but I never had the chance." Richter said, "You know, when I came to Wagner at Bayreuth, I had no experience, and he [Wagner] just trusted me and I learned it as I went along. I know you are a fine violinist and have played in your father's quartet, and you have played operas in Dresden. I know you are a good musician, and you will learn it as you go along. I will propose you as my successor here in Manchester." I nearly fell over! It was not a very good idea to tell me just before I had to go to the piano and play. (I think I was very nervous.) At night, you see, I lay in my bed and conducted the whole night. He did really propose me as his successor. But naturally, the committee said, "Oh, Petri, . . . first, he is a young man, then he is unknown, and has no routine as a conductor no, no, no, he is a pianist, we can't do that." So, they wouldn't have anything to do with me. Which was really foolish, because I would have become a very good conductor, I am sure.

The committee in Manchester finally engaged the son-in-law of Wagner. He had married one of the daughters (Winifred). His name was Ballin, as far as I remember. So, I missed one of the greatest chances of my life, for if I had stayed in Manchester, my entire life would have been altered. Well I don't know whether to be glad or sorry about it. I am really glad about it, I think. You see, a pianist is so independent. I go on to the stage, and no one has anything to say to me. I can do what I like. (Like Glen Gould but I wouldn't do that.) I know I used to say to my mother when I was about fourteen years old, "You know, I would like to conduct strings, and woodwinds, and brass, and that kind of thing. Only, I would not like to have anything to do with the men who play these instruments."

Here is just one more story, in which Egon figures as a conductor:

> There was Zdislaw Bernbaum in Warsaw (which means pear tree,
> not petri!). He was once late for a rehearsal and I was on time, and
> the orchestra was sitting there waiting for him. I was to play the
> Tchaikovsky. I thought he had been held up or his car had broken
> down. So, I thought, what's the use of wasting time here, so I said to
> the orchestra, "Why don't we just start. And then when he comes, he
> can take over." So, I gave the orchestra the notes of the horn (and
> then sneezed for the sforzando chords. Did you know that the Schu-
> mann begins with a sneeze, too? Of course, the Tchaikovsky is a
> regular hay-fever concerto!) No, really, I merely gave the horns their
> entrance, and then I sat down at the piano and played my D-flat ma-
> jor chords, and everything went very, very well and the orchestra en-
> joyed this very much. And then, Bernbaum came in. He looked very
> superciliously offended and looked at the stage. He took his baton
> and carried on, and he said to the orchestra, "Excuse me, I am con-
> ducting!" Very offended. You see, we could have played the whole
> thing without him quite easily. Bruno Walter has done it, and Bern-
> stein has done it. I heard him play the First Concerto of Beethoven
> and it went perfectly well. Mitropoulos has done it, too. And, at any
> rate, in the old days, the first violinist conducted with his bow, with
> his face to the audience and his back to the orchestra.

To sum up, then, Egon of necessity became, as each great pianist
must, his own best craftsperson, his own best musical interpreter, and
his own best *conductor*—these three always united as one.

Performing and Artistry

Gordon Watson, a Petri pupil in residence in Australia, relates that
Egon considered nervousness—whether due to concerns of the instrument, or whatever else—a form of egotism. "Don't think so much
of yourself and think more of the great things you are dealing with,"
Egon would say. (Granted, that can also make one nervous.)

Once, while walking a country path, Egon asked me, out of the blue, "Of course, you know where Sebastian Bach was born?" "Yes," I replied. "Ah, Eisenach [Germany]. . . . That means 'like iron,'" he continued. "Isn't it lovely that Bach, by destiny, had such strength of spirit." For Egon, the great composers were above all human beings, to be endlessly assessed, revered. "When all is said and done, it's best to just be the humble servant of the composer," he said. So, he was, and so we remember.

Regarding memorizing scores, Egon said, "There are five sources: 1. The eye, 2. The ear, 3. Finger movements ('the tactile senses'), 4. Construction (intervals, harmonies, tonalities), and 5. The form ('I know the form of it. . . . I know, for instance, when the second theme comes in the *Waldstein*, or the bridge passage, or the recapitulation, etc., etc.").

He continued, "I would really not rely on one of these things to the exclusion of the others. I would call upon one complex." Then came an extraordinary statement, given to emphasize the importance of the eye (no. 1) for memorization, in Egon's estimation: "I could write all the pieces which I ever played in my life in my concerts, in a room with no piano. Just give me a pen and paper, and I could write them down." Clarifying further, Egon reiterated, "In writing it down, you would call upon all the various senses in order to form your final version." Again, this seems more the conductor speaking than the instrumentalist.

A few words about Egon Petri's artistry. He had great presence, and although he seemed almost immobile sitting at the keyboard, his playing had deeply penetrative animation, vitality. Although each tone was made clear, a mellifluous whole would emerge, all lines instrumental, sonorous, melodious. The architecture of the music was always made clear, with a combination of boldness and subtlety. He seemed to distill complexities to their simplest essence, and only then portray and express the endless nuances. The effect in listening was to feel a kind of completeness. One heard rightness—appropriate, just. His recording of the slow movement of the "Hammerclavier" Sonata of Beethoven is an excellent example. A hallowed, balanced whole rises before the listener—insight through oversight.

The character and personality of each composition was cunningly wrought, without histrionics, an inner light; for example, the aura of retrospect, the play, the whimsy of Liszt's Ricordanza (the best recording of it ever made, APR 7701, disc 2); the demonism and innocence of Liszt's Mephisto (as Petri said, "First, peasant-heaviness, clumsiness, next innocence, and only then the smell of sulphur"); the liquid flow of the Schubert-Liszt lieder; the Germanic-Belgian yearning of Franck; the Italianate impetuosity of Liszt's Petrarch Sonnets; the epic lyricism of Chopin's sonatas; or the grandeur of Bach's "St. Anne" Prelude and Fugue. Jan Holcman touched upon a most rare aspect of Egon's artistry: "In Petri's performance of Busoni's Carmen Fantasy, the mutual nullifying traits of being both reserved and exciting exist simultaneously" (*Saturday Review*, 25 May 1972).

Especially in Petri's Beethoven, each composition was given its own composite character, each like none other, all characteristics derived from, and contributing to, that individual whole. Further, each subsidiary part of the form was imbued with its own relative, distinct values, its own charm. Transitions and cadenzas, especially, were invested with fresh, particular delights. For example, his Op. 10/2 of Beethoven expressed ebullient lyricism and mocking counterpoint; Op. 78, a cloth of lyrical embroidery; Op. 90, a pensive, autumnal colloquy and song; Op. 106, a vast symphonic Heldenleben saga; and Op. 111, a tale of demonic conflict, pilgrimage, and reverie.

While conversing on the subject of Beethoven, Egon once told us: "My father had a friend called Dr. Seymond, who lived in Bonn, where Beethoven was born. He lived in a three-storied house. One day, Seymond went up to the attic, probably not alone, with his servants, and told them to wrap up all these old papers with string, and sell them to the grocery store down the block, where they were used to wrap the herring and cheese. As he was supervising this packing, his eyes fell on some notes, and he pulled this paper out, and it was the original manuscript of Beethoven's Piano Sonata, Op. 26."

Jeremy Nicholas, in a review (*Gramophone,* December 2015) points out that Petri's recording of the "Hammerclavier" Op. 106 is "a commanding and properly monumental reading *to live with*" (my emphasis). Petri's performances were often indelible lifelong, a performance one would hold and compare with all others. Here then, through it all is Petri's nostalgic Lamp of Memory affixed to the evolving present in unending play.

Egon's live performances sometimes varied notably from his recordings. Tempi in the earlier recordings tend to be faster, for example. His performances on the recordings are, after all, only one instance of a vast chain of performances over many years. In some cases, though, for example, Franck's *Prelude, Chorale, and Fugue*, his interpretation remained remarkably constant over the years. All these recordings are *performances*, since Egon, during the process, never repeated works, or sections, or had splicing done on any of his record releases. What you hear is Egon performing each piece, straight through, once only. As related earlier, "When the time comes, you go out and you play on that piano, and do the very best you can." He was referring not only to his attitude toward the available instrument; he also meant you do your best at first and once. And you must be ready. Extraordinarily, through many, many years Egon was ready. Yet, he was never totally satisfied with a performance. He always admitted there was more he wanted, more to be done. (See footnote 32 and accompanying text.) Here again are his confidence and his humility entwined at the root.

And this: whenever Egon's fingers touched the keys, a sense of wonder would arise between performer and listener, as in a magician's sleight of hand, a conjurer's charm, confirmation of Petri's inborn affinities.

Egon Petri was a pianist, born and bred: by Fate, a musician; by Will, a master-interpreter; by Design, a disciple, maintained and nourished lifelong by conviction, determination, and love. There is no mold for such artists. If they pass by at all, they pass by but once.

Chapter 2

Influences

His [Petri's] remarkable fusion of transcendental virtuosity and sensitive musicality. . . .

Mark Ainley, 2015

It is always valuable to recall persons who had the strongest influence upon a great musician's ideals early in life. In Petri's case, in such a musically rich childhood, there were many. However, many decades later in my conversations with Egon, especially in 1961–1962, five people stood out: d'Albert, Paderewski, Anton Rubinstein, Busoni, and Egon's father Henri Wilhelm Petri.

Although Egon had little memory of Eugene d'Albert as a teacher, he had a vivid memory of d'Albert's playing. D'Albert was, after Tausig, considered Liszt's most brilliant pupil: "a dazzling talent," "our young Lion," said Liszt. D'Albert lived a tempestuous life, which included six wives (the first of whom was the volatile Teresa Carreño; d'Albert was her third husband). Later, d'Albert took almost exclusively to composing. Nevertheless, he was considered not only the greatest Beethoven pianist, but also the best all-round pianist and successor of Liszt.[19]

---

[19] Eugene d'Albert (1864–1932), born in Glasgow, Scotland, died in Riga, Latvia. English pianist and composer, son of a German dancing master (who wrote popular music). A child prodigy, he entered the New Music School in London at age ten. At seventeen, he played his own concerto with

As Petri recalled, "I have heard the G Major Concerto (of Beethoven) played by d'Albert, and I don't think it could be beaten by anybody now. It was just marvelous. It was warm and soulful . . . not intellectual. He had a beautiful touch and a beautiful clean technique."

During a Brahms festival in Leipzig in 1895 (on 31 January), d'Albert performed both Brahms concertos in a single concert, with Brahms conducting. (Egon was then fourteen years old.) Brahms considered d'Albert the finest interpreter of his piano music (even beyond von Bülow). D'Albert was then considered the preeminent interpreter of Beethoven and Brahms. In the midst of a continuously turbulent life, and incessant composing, d'Albert's artistry must have been of the very highest order.

Even if Petri's remembrances were colored by time, here was Beethovian artistry/musicianship that, throughout a long lifetime, remained for Petri foremost, ideal.

Regarding d'Albert's artistry and Petri's use of the term "intellectual," an explanation is needed. Petri recoiled against any undue, or extreme intellectual overlay in performance, whereby a performer, by his/her theories, ideals, or convictions ends by interfering with or distorting the natural flow of the music within its most intrinsic unfolding. Petri called such interference "intellectual," or "*too* intellectual."

Hans Richter. He was compared to Mendelssohn and Mozart. He received a Mendelssohn Scholarship for study in Vienna, then studied with Liszt. Later, he repudiated his English birth, adopting German citizenship. Appointed conductor at Weimar in 1907. He became director of the Hochschule in Berlin. Changing his name to the German form "Eugen," he sided with Germany during the First World War. Although he took to composing almost exclusively, he was renowned for his interpretations of Beethoven and Brahms. His compositions include two piano concertos, a string quartet, a symphony, an oratorio, and twenty operas. (The Library of Congress holds eleven d'Albert opera manuscripts.)

Petri's objection held whether such interference seemed justified or false. That doesn't mean Petri was anti-intellectual, for he admittedly used his intellect constantly in performance. ("Intellectual" was a term so used by Egon's father, especially against Busoni.) In the later 19th century, it was expected of a performer to be highly individual, personal, idiosyncratic. Under such circumstances, Petri was commending d'Albert most highly in declaring him "not intellectual," but rather a natural, unaffected, intuitive performer.

Ignace Jan Paderewski (1860–1941) also had a great impact upon young Egon. It's difficult to encompass the extent of Paderewski's fame which long permeated Europe and America. At one time he was even elected prime minister of Poland! Anyone and everyone knew who he was. Petri's father naturally turned to Paderewski when pondering his young son's future. As Petri said, "He (Paderewski) was very, very charming, a great artist and poet."

After hearing Egon play the piano, Paderewski advised a career as a pianist. As Egon said, "Paderewski's advice was really a turning point in my life. I had great admiration for him." However, of Paderewski's playing, Egon said, "Paderewski was very, very free . . . too free sometimes." For example, he suggested Egon take many more freedoms of tempo in his performance of the opening movement of Beethoven's Op. 109 (as did Busoni). Petri's conservative ideals at that moment may have come partially from his father's more fastidious approach. Even as a youth, then, Petri felt Paderewski's freedoms could become excessive. Later critics of Paderewski's playing could be scathing regarding these freedoms of tempo, rubato, expression, while the public's admiration never waned.

As Petri recalled, "I learned very much . . . that there is a very fine balance between playing too much in time and too much rubato." (Paderewski's rubato was both famous, and infamous.) "You can go too far. You mustn't obscure the meter by freedom of playing. It's not a question of this or that—but *how much*." Petri was to learn this from Busoni also.

Paderewski would greet Egon by saying, "Ohhh, Petri, son of my great friend Henri Petri!" They would speak Polish together. Of Paderewski, Egon would say "Others could say he [Paderewski] does not play octaves well." "In the Liszt Sonata, his octaves were like a bad pupil's," or "does not play the *piano* well—but he is a great artist and poet." As Petri recounted, "It wasn't the technique of Paderewski that attracted people and made him famous, but his personality, his charm, his poetry, his imagination, and all these things."

Mrs. K. and I have in our possession a recital program of Paderewski's, from 1917 in Boston. The first half opened with Beethoven's Sonata Op. 111, followed by Papillons of Schumann, and then Paderewski's own Sonata Op. 21. There is a report of one concert where Paderewski played the "Waldstein" and "Appassionata" sonatas of Beethoven, then the last three sonatas of Beethoven, Bach's Chromatic Fantasy and Fugue, and pieces by Chopin. He once played six concertos and three recitals in one week. It's not difficult to see that Egon's penchant for large programs originated from such influences. (See chapter 4, "Repertoire.")

To sum up, it remained an object lesson to Petri that, regardless of the magnetism of towering personality, charm, poetry, and imagination, things could still go wrong.

Another indelible influence upon young Egon was the immensely imposing Russian pianist Anton Rubinstein (1830–1894), then considered by many the greatest virtuoso after Liszt (a rival of d'Albert for that title). "Strength and lightness, these are the secrets of my touch," he declared. Rubinstein once explained to Rachmaninoff that his way was to "press upon the keys until the blood oozes from my fingertips"! Beginning at age ten, Egon recalled hearing Rubinstein perform ten times or more. Rubinstein's impact upon young Egon was immediate and total. "It was all so great, with a soft tone and beautifully planned architecturally, a powerful touch. . . . He could play like velvet and like steel."

Sometimes Rubinstein would be sloppy, or he would lose his place, but, Petri said, "It didn't matter, for everything he did was so great." "This titanic playing of Rubinstein, with all the greatness and all the expression and feeling; he didn't analyze it, but it just came out as if it were a volcano bursting. So, you didn't mind the wrong notes."

Edward Weiss, a pupil of Busoni, relates that Busoni had been a teacher at the Moscow Conservatory while Anton Rubinstein was there. One day Busoni and Wassily Safonoff were walking down the hall and they heard the most ravishing sounds coming from a practice room, and they went in. It was Rubinstein. Busoni told Weiss that Rubinstein's colors and tonal effects were the best he had ever heard. Anton Rubinstein was Busoni's favorite pianist. Busoni never heard Liszt in his prime. He heard Liszt once in Vienna when Liszt was sixty-six, having long before retired from playing in public. Busoni was bitterly disappointed. He thought the performance cold and uninspiring. Moreover, Liszt had injured a finger, and performed the "Emperor" Concerto of Beethoven with nine fingers only. (See Dent, *Ferruccio Busoni,* p. 24.)

I pause to compare these descriptions with three others: at age ten, in New York, I heard an electrifying recital by another Russian, Vladimir Horowitz, while at about the same age, Heidi Elfenbein in Los Angeles first heard the magisterial Artur Schnabel. In my case, the audience became unhinged, people shouted, cried, jumped up on their seats, or ran to the stage in a frenzy. In Mrs. K.'s case, absolute enduring stillness obtained, as awe and wonder arose and beatifically settled in. As Mrs. K. said, "No one moved, not even Schnabel." As for Petri, his concerts transpired more on the Schnabel side. It was as it is with the deepest listening experiences: first, the acute suspension in being spellbound; thereafter, rightful exhilaration and solace. Petri, like Schnabel, sat very still at the keyboard, always unperturbed,

while the music cascaded from the stage, seemingly of its own voli-
tion. Voices, harmonies, textures, colors abounded, emanations singular, yet somehow definitive, universal. In retrospect, perhaps the spirits of A. Rubinstein and Paderewski hover over such elemental
forces?

A serious composer, Rubinstein was also among the founders of
the St. Petersburg Conservatory (from 1861 on), giving regular "historical" recitals over the years for students. In the United States, he
once gave 215 concerts in 239 days, seven "farewell" historical programs in NYC in nine days. Much later, in St. Petersburg, each Sunday, for thirty-two weeks, Rubinstein gave a different program, with
lectures interspersed.

Rubinstein's enormous, far-ranging programs, too, were justly
famous. For example, the second of his "historical" recitals in America consisted of sonatas of Beethoven, "Moonlight," "Waldstein,"
"Appassionata," Op. 90, Op. 101, Op. 109, and Op. 111. His fourth
program, dedicated to Schumann, was this: Fantasy in C, Kreisleriana,
Etudes symphonique, Sonata in F-sharp, short pieces, and Carnaval.
Inexplicably, Rubinstein was always considered a legendary pupil of
Liszt. This was an erroneous assumption, since Liszt never accepted
him as a pupil, a rare and puzzling case. Above all, Petri remembered
the unparalleled impact of Rubinstein's artistry, its dazzling poetry, its
endless colors, its volcanic force.

Ferruccio Busoni (1866–1924) was certainly a crucial influence
upon young Egon. Petri was drawn to his charisma, riveting pianism,
wide education, analytical powers, fierce intellect, and visionary ideals. (See Dent's *"Ferruccio Busoni*, and Busoni's treatise, *Sketch of a
New Aesthetic of Music* (1907).) Busoni long considered himself a
composer of Mozartian potential. Busoni longed for a realm of "Good
and Great Universal Music," where all instruments "resonate together
and at once, carry you, entwine themselves round you, brush against
you—melodies of love and sorrow, of spring and winter, of melan-

choly and high spirits . . . the feelings of a million beings in a million epochs." (See also Antony Beaumont, *Busoni the Composer*, and Beaumont, *Selected Letters of Busoni*, the latter chosen from fifty thousand extant letters.)

Busoni's influence upon Egon was multifarious. "I owe most of my introduction to literature to Busoni. . . . He gave me [Hans Christian] Anderson stories when I was a boy. He introduced me to George Bernard Shaw, to [Edgar Allen] Poe, to ETA Hoffmann, and all the German romantics."

As for Busoni's pianism, Egon said, "Busoni was intellectual(!) and architectural." "Busoni liked the Liszt brilliant playing. His idea was *not* to play beautifully with expression." Egon's father said, "Busoni was like the Snow Queen by Anderson, all glittery with ice and rainbow colors . . . and cold." Busoni's attitudes were certainly patrician, aristocratic: he said there are only two possible environments for piano playing, the concert hall and the private practice room.

On first going to Busoni's class in 1900 at age twenty in Weimar, Egon recounted, "Busoni gave wonderful recitals at this masterclass. Busoni played many pieces of Liszt that were little known, such as the Benediction. His playing was marvellous. Naturally, I learned a lot." Apparently, Busoni's playing was always sculpted, pristine, mindful.

In an article in 1940 entitled "How Ferruccio Busoni Taught" (in the *Etude Magazine*, October 1940), Petri wrote: "When Busoni played, the most surprising sounds emerged from the piano. They resembled sounds one would expect from a wind instrument rather than from a percussion instrument. His Mozart—a composer for whom he had the greatest admiration—was the most limpid flowing stream of sound I have ever heard. One felt as if he, you and the piano might be floating." "For Busoni, the paramount thing was the big line—flowing and unified."

Although Busoni had a comprehensive technique which could be dazzling, Petri said, "He (Busoni) did not like a big or overpowering tone and always played with the lid of the piano closed." Of the pedals, Egon recalled, "Busoni used them very little, and expected the same of his pupils." Further, Egon recalled, "But, his (Busoni's) playing was never the same. At one time it left the listener quite cold, and at another, it lifted him to the skies."

Marta Weigert, a pupil of Busoni who attended the Weimar masterclasses in 1901, concurred: "During the following weeks he (Busoni) sometimes played one or two of Liszt's greatest compositions in the Tempelherrenhaus (Goethe's old haunt, lent to Busoni by the Duke of Weimar, also once inhabited by Liszt). So, I heard for the first time in my life the 'Dante' Sonata, Etudes Transcendentes, many of the opera Fantasias and also parts of 'Pelerinage d' Italie' and 'Pelerinage de Suisse.' We had a rather limited knowledge of Liszt, and to hear his music played with such unimaginable perfection and beauty was overwhelming to us (class members)."

Weigert first met Busoni in Cologne, where she had auditioned for him, performing Chopin's G Minor Ballade. After talking about her performance for a while, she relates, Busoni "suddenly sat down at the piano and began to play the last 'presto furioso' of the 'Ballade,' giving the left hand strong accents and increasing the excitement with unbelievable dynamic power up to the scales at the end which he played like a thunderstorm." Thereafter, he said, 'If you support the right hand more with the left (thus anchoring the syncopations),' he explained calmly, 'you will get less tired and your interpretation will become much more effective. You have to plan the economy of your own strength. Come to Weimar with an open mind, and there you will hear more about all this.'" (Marta Weigert, "Busoni at Weimar in 1901," *The Music Review*, 1954.)

Once, in conversation with Rudolph Serkin in Marlboro, Mrs. K and I mentioned Busoni. Serkin placed his hands together as in prayer, as he often did for important matters, and intoned "Busoni was always clean. All others were sometimes dirty, but Busoni was *always clean*!"

"But," said Egon, "Busoni sometimes took such liberties. He sometimes went too far." More, "He didn't want to play in time and sometimes you couldn't even hear where the tempo was." "There was a conductor in Berlin who in a rehearsal with Busoni of a Mozart piano concerto suddenly put down his baton, exclaiming, 'Such playing cannot be accompanied,' and left the stage. "As well, in Chopin, he did absolutely crazy things!" "Busoni was determined to be original, to do something no one else would do, to change the music, alter it, improve it." "He even re-wrote some of Schönberg's piano pieces. Schönberg was furious!"

On the other hand, being original in a different way, Busoni once collaborated with Mahler to remove all "traditional" perform-ance conventions from the "Emperor" Concerto of Beethoven, to de-velop a new, fresh interpretation derived only from the score alone. Thus Busoni went beyond Mahler's potent dictum, "Tradition is tend-ing the flame, not worshipping the ashes."

Edward Weiss, another pupil of Busoni, once said that he felt that although Busoni considered himself to be the best pianist alive(!), he was never satisfied with himself. Once, in rehearsing a Mozart concerto for performance with the Berlin Philharmonic, Weiss relates that he, as pianist, and Busoni, as conductor, rehearsed every day for three months! Each day Busoni would have a new idea, wanting to change something, to try a new approach. As Weiss said, "I was des-perate!"

Busoni would say arresting or strange things, for example, "There is no modern or old, but only good and bad music." And "Tal-ent has nothing to do with intelligence whatsoever." Egon's father considered Busoni paradoxically a very intelligent mind but not a very fine musician, whereas Busoni considered Henri Petri neither a fine mind nor a fine musician. Egon mused, "Busoni was much more for analyzing than for the music." But, by his admission, Busoni later indicated that he had changed when he said, "Nowadays, the expression of a face is more important to me than its lines." As Petri recalled, "Busoni was the one who put Mozart above Beethoven. However, he did not put Haydn above Mozart, which I do sometimes."

Busoni could be playful, as Egon recounted, unusual for that time. Busoni had performed the Beethoven piano concertos using Beethoven's own cadenzas. A critic wrote, "The concerto was played very beautifully, but the cadenzas of Busoni were absolutely out of style." Busoni rang the critic up at 7 o'clock in the morning at his home—the critic was just getting out of bed—and Busoni spoke very deeply over the phone, "Hier Beethoven, die Cadenzen von *mir*!" ("This is Beethoven. The cadenzas are *mine*!")

(Petri had his own adventures with critics, as when a critic wrote a review of an early orchestral composition written by him "Petri should leave off performing—Petri has absolutely no talent for composing." (!) Egon explained, "They had my Nocturne on the program, but they substituted Debussy's Nocturne, since they couldn't prepare mine in time. So, the critic was really reviewing Debussy, thinking it was me.")

There was the time that Busoni, Petri, and Edward Weiss went together to the Beethovensaal in Berlin to hear Eugene d'Albert. The playing was full of mistakes (perhaps by now, d'Albert, wholly engaged in his composing, was neglecting his performing skills.) Nevertheless, Busoni thought the performance magnificent. Suddenly turning to Egon, Busoni said, "If only *you* could make such mistakes!"

Another time Petri mused, "If you had asked d'Albert about Busoni, he would have said, 'Well, he is just one of those calculating, paradoxical people. He is not a real born musician.' And he would have been right!" In a deeply pensive mood, Petri once confided, "Busoni was not interested in the pupil. Not ever! Not me either!"

This shocked Petri, who was *always* interested in, and concerned about, his students. Equally dire, this: "Busoni was not a teacher." And this: "He (Busoni) was a man who deceived himself and others." Summing up, Petri declared "I certainly never 'studied' with Busoni. All he would say was that I played 'beautifully.' And from Busoni, that was no compliment."

Egon Petri, from the cover of an EMI record released in 1967, *Egon Petri: Piano Music by Beethoven, Busoni, Liszt.* Great Instrumentalists Series No. 7.

Nevertheless, even late, Petri would muse: "For many years, in fact even sometimes now, I do not know what is Busoni and what is mine." Another time he said, "Busoni was undoubtedly the greater person and intellect and pianist, but I sometimes think I am the better musician." (This said with Petri's inevitable blend of pride and humility). "But," he once reminisced, "I was a young man (of twenty or so) and shy and too much in awe of him and his authority." Regardless of all this, when Busoni died in 1924, Petri said simply, "We wept, for we loved him very much."

Even in the 1930s, long after Busoni's death in 1924, Egon was still widely known as a disciple of Busoni, regularly being asked to perform Busoni's gigantic piano concerto (in five huge movements, ending with a male chorus, text from Oehlenschlager's "Aladden").

Petri had played this concerto several times under Busoni's baton in the capitals of Europe. Of his early years, Egon said, "But nobody played as much like Busoni as I did. . . . But I think I have combined two different worlds . . . the brilliant Liszt conception of piano playing, and then to make real music, which doesn't always go together."

As postscript here, there is the story of Edward Steurmann in Los Angeles, who was about to perform an evening of Schönberg's piano music. Backstage, Steurmann paced back and forth. Schönberg asked, "Why are you pacing so?" Steurmann replied, "I am nervous." "But," said Schönberg, "You know the music so well." "No," said Steurmann, "I'm afraid I'll make a mistake." "Oh, don't worry," said Schönberg, "and anyway, everyone makes mistakes." "No, that isn't true," said Steurmann, "*Busoni*! Busoni never makes mistakes!" "Oh, Busoni," answered Schönberg, "Well, he doesn't count. . . . And besides, he does that on purpose!"

All sources seem to confirm that Busoni was a dominating musician and teacher, though not the immortal composer and theorist he hoped to be. Certainly, Petri learned much, though Busoni's legacy ended by being so Janus-faced. Even if Busoni was definitively "great on purpose," he was great nonetheless.

Last to be considered here is Petri's father, the violinist Henri Wilhelm Petri (1856–1914), originally from Utrecht, Holland. (In Utrecht, one of two musician brothers of Henri eventually formed a Petri Music School.) As a precocious orphaned teen, Henri was recommended to King Wilhelm III of Holland, who gave Henri a scholarship to study in Berlin with the renowned Joseph Joachim, then the most famous violinist in Europe.[20] Henri was eventually recognized as one of the finest pupils of Joachim. Lifelong, said Egon, "Joachim was very fond of my father." In Berlin, Henri soon met his future

---

[20] Joseph Joachim (1831–1907) was the preeminent German violinist, an unexcelled soloist and chamber musician. A lifelong friend of Brahms, he first performed in public at age seven. At age ten, he was sent to the Vienna Conservatory, and at age twelve he performed in Leipzig with Mendelssohn accompanying; afterward he was soloist with the Gewandhaus Orchestra. He toured England at age thirteen, and frequently thereafter, becoming concertmaster of the Weimar Orchestra at age twenty-three. The Hochschule für Musick was opened in Berlin in 1868 with Joachim as director. He formed the Joachim String Quartet in 1869. Joachim premiered Brahms' Violin Concerto, New Year's Day, 1879. In 1882–1887, he was one of the principal conductors of the Berlin Philharmonic. He was considered the most imposing violin teacher in Europe. Joachim received many honorary degrees from German universities and various orders of knighthood. Gradually, Joachim became as great a conductor as violinist. "His style of playing, nurtured on the best Classical models, was remarkable for masterful repose, dignity, and flawless technique" (*Baker's Dictionary*). Joachim's compositions for violin are "virtuoso pieces that have never ceased to attract performers" (*Baker's*). Among his compositions are two violin concertos, chamber pieces, several overtures, and cadenzas for the violin concertos of Beethoven and Brahms, besides songs. Brahms predicted a brilliant career for Joachim as a composer, a career to be far greater than Brahms' own. Joachim was cruelly disappointed when Petri did not become his pupil in 1901, and seems to have resented this refusal lifelong.

wife, Kathi, a member of a musical family with whom Henri was rooming. Kathi's father was second violinist in the Berlin State Opera Orchestra, as I said.

Henri's career is outlined in chapter 1, "Youth," where I mentioned that he was the distinguished concertmaster in Leipzig and Dresden, leader of a renowned string quartet, soloist, and chamber musician, even premiering works of Brahms in Dresden.

Free and almost profligate in his teens ("Early, my father was very easy with his money—that I have also inherited"), he later became a highly frugal, deliberate, disciplined person. "My father was a very precise, tidy man, and one of his ideas was never to waste anything," recalled Egon. All during Egon's childhood, his father set aside all his loose change, so that years later, when Egon was about to leave home, his father presented him with the equivalent of five hundred dollars, as a going away present.

"Brahms gave me a piece of candy for my fifth birthday. My father didn't give it to me, which I think is very cruel, but rather wrapped it up in paper, tied it 'round with a note, 'Given to Egon on his 5th Birthday by Johannes Brahms.' When I left home, he gave it to me."

Another peculiarity: "My father always read newspapers, but never books. He said, 'The newspaper is the best novel in the world.'" However, as Egon added, "I have done precisely the opposite. I read only books, never newspapers. . . . I'm sure that if there were a war, or someone dropped an atom bomb, my students would tell me."

As concertmaster, Egon's father was formidable: "My father was very strict. No one in the orchestra was allowed to cross his legs. He had jurisdiction over the orchestra in these matters, and they were afraid of him. They respected him, but they also feared him."

But, Henri Petri could also be generous. For example, he helped young Busoni (at age twenty) by offering him hospitality, giving Busoni a key to his apartment (as a "continuous guest"), even helping Busoni financially. As Egon recalled, "It was called borrowing, but Busoni never paid anything back." (Later, Busoni also lent money he never expected to be returned.) Young Busoni almost caused a serious rift by refusing to play for Joachim during an evening in the Petri home. Busoni simply disliked Joachim. (Dent, *Ferruccio Busoni*, p. 80) How shocked Henri must have been later, when Busoni announced to Henri's beautiful wife Kathi that he was in love with her, and meant to divorce his wife and marry her!

All his life, Egon's father kept a special keepsake close: "King Wilhelm of Holland gave my father upon his departure for Berlin (to study with Joachim) a gold watch which has a French inscription, 'By a special watchmaker to the King of Holland.' It is a Swiss watch. I still have it standing on my desk and it is a wonderful timekeeper."

Egon, late in life, had such laudable things to say about his father's musicality: "My father had a very, very elegant manner of playing the violin, and he looked very noble and everyone used to admire him." In fact, "Everybody admired him so, the English colony (in Dresden) and the American colony, and I think they were all in love with my father and his playing. . . . My father was a very precise, tidy man. My father was very strict." Musically speaking, "My father had a very good sense of rhythm, and a beautiful tone. I played the D minor Brahms violin sonata with him, and I have never played with anybody with whom I was so happy. I don't think anybody has played it more beautifully." (See chapter 1, "Youth," for a description of Egon performing this sonata with his frequent collaborator Joseph Szigeti.)

"My father used much portamento," Petri recalled, "a rising curve to the note. Used in slight measure, it is very nice. Singers do it. It can be a very warm expression. But, when done too much, then it seems as if one sends a searchlight out for the note. . . . Then I am glad the piano can't do it!" Then Petri added "But, the piano can suggest it (a portamento) by a very warm tone, and by holding the keys down, and overlapping, and carefully selecting the dynamics of the tones in question."

"My father had a tiny little French flair in his Dutch-German playing," recalled Egon. "Otherwise, my father kept to the tempo . . . almost too much."

"My father was what was known then as a 'Brahmin' (a Brahms devotee)," he said once, continuing, "He played the three Brahms Violin Sonatas [also with Egon accompanying on the piano] and was the first to play the three Brahms String Quartets in Dresden" (with Henri Petri's string quartet, of which Egon was sometimes second violinist). Once, Egon confided to me, "My father thought I was the best second violinist he had ever had."

Brahms was a personal friend of the family, visiting the Petri home on numerous occasions. During Brahms' last year, the Petris visited Brahms in Vienna to solicit advice regarding Egon's future, whether or not Egon should finish school before inaugurating a musical career. Brahms advised the parents to let Egon finish school as insurance against an unknown future. Brahms respected and admired Henri Petri as a musician, and as a person. The younger Petri said, "As a boy I lapped up Brahms' music like mother's milk, and I loved it and never doubted it." "The Brahms D minor Concerto: I played it at home even before I had 'studied' with Busoni." All under his father's Brahmsian wing!

Egon commented that "Busoni didn't like him (Brahms). He thought him too thick and too German . . . too heavy-blooded. . . . That was the Italian in him [Busoni]." Egon was to hear another kind of violin playing in 1902 at age twenty-one when he heard Eugene Ysaye, the great Belgian virtuoso, perform the Beethoven Concerto in Berlin. "He was the only one Busoni admired. Busoni didn't like my father's playing and he didn't like Joachim's, either. It was too 'academic' and too regular for him," Egon recalled.

"Ysaye had a wonderful freedom in his playing. . . . It wasn't so set and regular as I was used to hear it. So I admired him very much." Egon was introduced to Ysaye by Busoni after the concert. He stared at Egon, then intoned "Du must arbeit!" ("You must work!").[21] "Busoni played with Ysaye quite a bit," Egon recalled later. "I heard Ysaye play the Beethoven Concerto and I said to my friends, 'It was like a meadow of flowers—so beautiful in colors.'" Edward Dent, in

---

[21] Eugene Ysaye was born in Liège, Belgium in 1858 and died in Brussels in 1931. He was a formidable personage. Egon recounted an incident about Ysaye told to him by Busoni: "Ysaye had written a cadenza for the Beethoven Violin Concerto. He played it in some town and a young man came to him afterwards and said, 'Maestro, it was wonderful—your playing of the Beethoven Concerto, but you know, I didn't like the cadenza. I didn't think it was in style.' 'What,' said Ysaye, 'you don't like the cadenza?' and he slapped the young man in the face. It is impudence for a young man to say this, who is a nobody. To tell this to his face! What does Ysaye care whether he likes the cadenza. He hasn't been asked. If Ysaye had said to Busoni, 'How do you like my cadenza' that would be another thing."

Ysaye had a long, phenomenal international career, as violinist, chamber musician, quartet leader, and conductor. Also as a composer, he wrote eight violin concertos, six violin sonatas, considerable chamber music, and an opera in the Walloon language. César Franck dedicated his Violin Sonata to Ysaye in 1886 as a wedding present. Debussy dedicated his String Quartet to the Ysaye String Quartet and Ysaye in 1893. Ysaye's favorite Guarnerius, made in Cremona in 1740, is now famously known as the "Ysaye Guarnerius." Long after Ysaye's death, it was purchased by Isaac Stern in 1965, thereafter becoming Stern's favorite instrument. The year Ysaye died, he placed a label inside his violin: "This del Gesu has been the faithful companion of my career." Late in Stern's life, he added a label: "Mine, too." Stern has written, "If I were given the opportunity to hear any two violinists in the entire history of the instrument, I would choose without hesitation, Paganini and Ysaye."

his fulsome biography of Busoni, relates that "Ysaye had Rubinstein's laugh, and Rubinstein's mixture of animalism, vulgarity, and kingliness" (p. 124). But, there was also more.

Nevertheless, lifelong, Egon admired his father's artistry. The ideal was to keep caringly to a chosen tempo, keep accurate and subtle rhythms, portray meanings faithfully, make the architecture clear, find the spirit, the soul, the personality of each individual composition (rather according to Joachim and Brahms), ennobling all without falsity or bombast. Egon's father ended by being right about Busoni's mannerisms, about d'Albert's peerless artistry, about interpreting Brahms, and music in general. Petri summarized it thus: "I think I have combined my father's innate musical feeling and interpretation with Busoni's pianism." And this: "I was very proud of my father." For his father, to be at the service of each composer was a sacred duty. The son, like the father, ended in essential concurrence—a rare artistic incidence of "like father, like son."

Postscript

Regarding memory and recall, scientists now know that seemingly fixed memories irrevocably undergo alterations and reappraisals over time, that maintaining a "fixed" memory is seemingly not possible. (Is there any truth in William James's theory that when we remember something we're really remembering our memory of it?) Even in attempting to keep a memory or an image pristine, a human will even, in the act of memorializing it, color it, simplify it, or enhance it. What is notable, regarding the above five special influences, is Egon's attitudes concerning his recollections fifty or sixty years later: most are recalled quite openly as personal remembrances, subjective—yet also objective. Egon seems always to have arrived at an instinctive balance which allowed him to artistically appreciate, even revere, but also to judge substance, worth, impact, an inestimable quality so necessary for any great artistic endeavor. These same attributes served him valiantly in all his years of teaching.

Bear in mind, too, that Egon's early memories were formed before the advent of audio recordings. If one wanted to hear a musical composition in those days, one either heard someone perform it, or one performed it oneself. The human memory was, during these times, as during all former written and unrecorded history, the only "audio-recording device." Such a restriction surely must have helped vitalize Egon's depth of recall.

We, with all our Babel-towers of recordings and endless Internet streaming, must try to re-enter those times, however difficult or impossible, when considering and reconsidering any of Egon's memories, experiences, remarks.

Chapter 3

Teaching

You can't help being your own teacher and pupil when you practice.

Egon Petri

Once you figure out what's wrong, there are no difficulties.

Egon Petri

Widely recognized as a virtuoso, Petri was also justly acknowledged as a great teacher, first in Europe, then in America.

Although devoted, principled, he nevertheless remained unaffected, cheerful, urbane. His kindness and generosity were always present, his humor irrepressible. He never turned his irony or sarcasm toward personal insult or harm. (Bear in mind that, in Petri's time, contrarily, European teachers, especially Russian and German, regularly taught by intimidation and deliberate humiliation.) Petri held an easy authority, since we all knew he had masterfully performed an enormous amount of the standard repertory, including over forty concertos. To the end, he retained daunting powers of technical mastery and recall. He seemed to remember every piece he had ever studied. His sessions usually combined detailed technical advice with musical and psychological information, tempered by the necessary historical outlook. In lessons overall, life would become an open book.

Lifelong, Petri investigated the various teaching "methods," each in turn, such as Deppe, Leschetizky, Matthay, Breithaupt, and finally, Ortmann, Schultz, and Whiteside. Those methods of Ludwig Deppe and Theodor Leschetizky were already out in the world during Egon's youth. He also took note of those ideas of Tobias Matthay and

Rudolf Breithaupt as they first appeared, Matthay's publications in the years 1903–1913, and Breithaupt's, in 1905–1909. Later, Egon considered Otto Ortmann and Arnold Schultz especially imposing pedagogues, Ortmann's epochal work appearing in 1929, and Schultz's in 1936. Abby Whiteside's ideas, holistic in the main, emerged gradually during this time.

Petri considered a single teaching "method" impossible, since, as he said, each student is different in thinking and acting, and each student's equipment or lack of equipment so highly individual. He agreed with Leschetizky that the only proper "method" is to teach each pupil individually. Despite the accounts of several of Leschetizky's students, Petri often invoked Leschetizky himself as declaring there was no "Leschetizky method."

Petri remained deeply skeptical of the many current "theories" of piano playing. One by one, he fought through the many artificial strictures, false proscriptions, and illusions within absolute "rules" or "methods." His early teacher, Böhm, taught Egon the Czerny exercises, "knuckles low, fingers high, wrist loose." Later, Teresa Carreño demanded "finger-lifting, strong and slow," with fifty or one hundred repetitions of each task. She said, "Egon, you must be able to carry a glass of water on your hand." As Petri observed, "Her movements were so spare she didn't think she moved at all." Some teachers then were advocating practicing while holding books under one's arms. No wonder Petri felt fortunate that he was "lazy," and did not do all his teachers asked of him. "For," he said, "I might well have been ruined!" He meant this seriously.

Looking back, Petri ruminated, "I didn't know at all about the keys (speed of the key). I had to find out for myself, because nobody really taught me the piano."

Besides his innate gifts, it was Egon's pragmatism, his independence, his curiosity, his determination, that saved him. In fact, all these things helped him to become a great teacher.

Petri felt it most curious that, during his early professional years, teachers seemed to be discovering *fingers* anew (like Deppe, who demanded very curved fingers, which should "fall on the keys," and "fall on chords," everything slow, slow, slow).[22] Petri said, "Everything then was fingers! Fingers had to be lifted high, knuckles low, like German goose-stepping." Petri often hypothesized that this restrictive, easily harmful approach originated with the autocratic Frederick Wieck, Clara Schumann's stern father. More, Breithaupt declared that "the hand is built like the spokes of a wheel." Petri would respond that "no wheel-spokes could perform the finale of the 'Appassionata' Sonata of Beethoven!"

Petri discovered for himself the notable differences of each finger, the third finger slow and strong, the second finger, fleet and light, the fourth finger, quite agile if not required to first lift before striking, and the fifth finger, firm, which often likes to flick without much curving. It is up to the pianist to treat each one kindly and sensibly in order to form an effective unified playing unit.

Petri had also discovered the three ways the thumb works: (1) down and up; (2) away and toward the hand; (3) as part of the hand. In scale playing, Egon objected strongly to the requirement that the thumb always be tucked under the hand early, and always curved. In rapid scales, for example, the thumb might not go under the hand much, or at all, since the hand itself is moving so rapidly. And sometimes, the thumb might go *over* the hand, as in the rapid thirds in the B-flat Concerto of Brahms.

Further, teachers would speak of "positions," whereas Petri taught continuity of motions, where no fixed position is possible, or

---

[22] See Amy Fay, *Music Study in Germany*, 1880, a charming young American's insightful account of piano studies with Tausig, Liszt, Kullak, and Deppe.

where there is no safety in positions, only safety in continuity of movement.

In turn, attention moved to discovering the pianist's *forearm*, and "arm weight" (Matthay, 1903–1913). Petri considered arm weight alone rather limited; for often, the forearm must be "light," mobile and quick. Petri would say, "The forearm is often light, sometimes briefly heavy, but usually moving the hand and fingers to the next keys. Arcs and circles abound." (Using weight alone, one can soon lose accuracy in faster or rapid passages.)

Next came the *upper* arm: when Petri came to his first teaching position in Manchester, England in 1905, he found some students who were required to hold books under their upper arms! Petri believed that practice chimerical. Without engaging the upper arm, the farther, outer ranges of the keyboard are impossible to reach. Only the upper arm can move the elbow, for example. Petri would declare, "It's remarkable that the upper arm rarely goes down, always out and back." With the elbow far away from the body, the upper arm can be practically parallel to the floor. "Sometimes," Egon would say, "arm weight can be our enemy."

Lastly came special attention to the *torso*, or "buttocks" (Abby Whiteside). However, Petri had long ago quickly come to the idea that in piano playing one is most often using *everything*—fingers, wrist, forearm, elbow, upper-arm, torso, as well as mind and spirit, in a unified continuum.

Petri objected to the words "wrist," "elbow," "shoulder." He would say, "Always say 'finger,' 'hand,' 'forearm,' since the wrist, elbow and shoulder are essentially conduits." Moreover, early in his career, Petri alone seemed to mention "rotation" and "lateral movements." They only entered the general conversation later.

Of all this historical journey through the pianist's playing units, Egon said, "Of course, I begin with the key, then I go to the fingers, then I proceed to the forearm, the upper-arm being only the steering mechanism." And "There is only the speed of the key." The retort would follow directly: "However, the mind comes first."

You can see, Dear Reader, that Petri became a formidable detective, a solver of difficulties, even riddles. Of technical problems, he would often say, "You make your own difficulties. Once you figure out what's wrong, there are no difficulties." (Granted, in such a solitary process, it is a great help to be Egon Petri.)

It's important to remember that everything Egon Petri suggested regarding musicianship and technique had been tested and honed on the firing line of experience—performance, practice, teaching, experimentation.

To Mrs. K. and myself, in all our years of teaching, Egon's ideas have remained practical, and as true as when he first taught us. Egon's solutions were so often a deft blend of science and art, a synthesis both pragmatic and spirited, with love permeating. As Leonardo da Vinci said, "The supreme misfortune is when theory outstrips performance."

This is the place to compare Petri's teaching with Busoni's. It has often been observed that most musicians teach as they were taught. Yet, although Petri was so much under the influence of Busoni at age twenty and twenty-one in Weimar (1901–1902), Petri's teaching had already considerably altered from Busoni's model by the time Petri arrived in Manchester in 1905. For example, Busoni held "sessions," whereas Petri gave "lessons." Busoni usually heard pieces only once, while Petri would hear a piece as often as necessary. Busoni never taught technique, Petri constantly taught the many aspects of technique, in his own pragmatic way, without theories, "rules," or "methods." Busoni, when possible, taught by indirect means, talking of composers, the music, the times, history, philosophy, literature,

Cover of record album, *Egon Petri Plays Beethoven*, issued circa 1960 by Westminster. Photo by Maria Martel. The inscription reads, "To my dear friends, Heidi and Al / affectionately / Egon."

sometimes performing to illustrate a point. Petri taught by direct method, addressing the specific composition, the particular problem in the actual place in the music. Busoni was not happy to be interrupted or contradicted; Petri always welcomed questions. Both illustrated with performance. As we see, then, each taught according to his own character and personality.

Busoni was patrician, reserved, though he was sometimes passionate, unpredictable, generous, and often indirect, even mysterious. (I speak here of Busoni's freer avenues—the master classes and private sessions, not his necessarily more traditionally oriented duties at the conservatories in Moscow, Basel, Boston, Helsinki, Vienna, and the Berlin Hochschule.) Petri, on the other hand, was always direct, cordial, pragmatic, probing, comprehensive. He could be mysterious, too, in the sources of his innovative solutions, and his steady application of surprising aphorisms and maxims.

At the summer Weimar master classes in 1901 and 1902, for example, Busoni would hold sway over twenty to thirty students. As Petri said, "In one afternoon, perhaps a dozen pupils would play, and at other times only two. Busoni would permit the person who was playing to go right through the piece without stopping for details. He never taught technique." (See article, Egon Petri, "How Furruccio Busoni Taught," *Etude Magazine*, October 1940.)

As Petri recalled, "It took quite a little time for someone to find sufficient courage to sit down at the piano first. Very often it was I, since knowing him so well made it somewhat easier. I was therefore nicknamed 'Egon the Reliable.'" More, "Taking lessons at his own home was an unpredictable thing. You could never make a definite appointment, but you could come to visit him, a visit which might or might not end in playing. Whatever the outcome, one was always sure to come away the richer. It may have been only a remark he made, a book he showed, or a phrase he played, that sent you off into hitherto unexplored regions and undreamed visions." As stated earlier, by Petri's estimate, he played to Busoni not more than a dozen times in thirty-eight years.

Petri noted, "His [Busoni's] own respect for the printed page was another trait which he impressed upon us. He would approach a work as if he had never seen it before, for the simple reason that he wanted to view it without preconceived notions. It was only in this way that he could best understand a composer's meaning, which to him was tantamount to a substitution of one's own personality." Petri's ideals were, overall, quite similar. (It's been noted earlier that Busoni could diverge sharply from these ideals, as well.)

As Petri said, Busoni "insisted that without knowing all of Beethoven, you could not sit down at the piano and profess to really understand the 'Appassionata' Sonata." One way or another, Petri declared, over all, "Busoni succeeded in equipping his students with that most valuable possession—independence of thought and spirit."

Summing up, Petri said, "I myself received an evaluation of art which it can be truthfully said, on looking backward, could not have been obtained in any other way. Busoni's ideas and personality determined my directions and growth to such an extent, that it is certain I would not be the same pianist if somehow there had not been this opportunity to study with him. The manner in which my taste and judgment were developed is due to him, as well as the knowledge that technique is a matter of intelligence and coordination, not of mechanics. I also learned to see music as a whole, in its broadest aspects of both forms and periods, together with its minutest details and various relationships." "Although we received only as much from this spiritual and intellectual communication as each of us was capable of absorbing, his brilliant insight into the life and form of a composition, his rounded knowledge of historical and aesthetic questions and his profound belief in ideal, unalterable concepts, could not help but give even to the least of us a more complete and knowing outlook."

Marta Weigert, a pupil of Busoni, keenly relates some of her adventures in the Weimar classes in her article "Busoni at Weimar in 1901" (*The Music Review*, 1954):

For me, the youngest amongst them, everything was new, strange and exciting; it took weeks 'til I adjusted myself and felt freer, since I was very shy. However, when at the first lesson Busoni asked us to play and nobody dared to, I found that they were all shy! Busoni looked around half laughing and half annoyed, until his eyes fell on Egon Petri: "But you, Egon, will you play?" Egon, with a boyish nod of his head, walked to the piano and shrugged his shoulders as if to say—"if it can't be helped then I have to play." If my memory does not fail me, he played Liszt's variations on Bach's "Weinen, Klagen." He played with great calmness, with controlled tone and technique. Busoni listened intently without interrupting and smiled sometimes when he liked a phrase especially well. When Petri had finished Busoni was very enthusiastic. "Very good," he repeated several times, "excellent." Then he discussed with Egon some works for future study.

Marta Weigert recalls how Busoni's students would voluntarily, privately help each other. For example, she relates,

A few weeks later it was again my turn to play. I brought Beethoven's Concerto in G which I had studied for only a short time, as Busoni had asked me to play something that was fairly new to me. This time he interrupted me frequently. He disagreed with some of my interpretations and asked for more powerful dynamics, a stronger and more even tone. To achieve this, he made me play some of the passages without any emotional expression but in a soft tone and asked me to watch and listen for the musical lines and their beauty. . . .

The next day Petri came to visit me. "You had a fine lesson yesterday," he remarked. "Now go on and practice." I was very low-spirited. "I think I shall have to give up entirely." He looked at me in amazement. "What a funny person you are. Is that your attitude to everything—all or nothing?" "May be," I said gloomily. Petri did not answer, but went to the piano and played the beginning of the G Major Concerto after the first *tutti*. I listened more and more intently and when he stopped I begged, "Please go on." I met a new kind of Beethoven—Busoni's Beethoven which I had not understood the day before. I was developing new ears for many things. Petri's touch was full and strong, but never hard. His interpretation was simple and without any sentimentality, never exaggerated, but sounding clear and beautiful. [Perhaps there was already also some of d'Albert's and Egon's Beethoven therein.] I was encouraged and filled with new interest, and made up my mind to do everything I could to play the Concerto better the following week. Petri and I began to discuss technical problems and went into many details. There was a wonderful spirit of helpfulness and interest amongst some of the pupils. And Petri became a most helpful friend.

There were lighter moments: at the end of the Weimar master classes in the summer of 1901, the students all accompanied Busoni to the train station. There, on the steps, was an old, ragged Gypsy playing his violin, his hat on the ground, begging for money. It took a while for Busoni and the class to realize it was Egon Petri.

Like Petri, Marta Weigert agrees that "the greatest influence of Busoni as a teacher was in the universality of his way of broadening our minds and our horizons about musical opinions and taste. He wanted to free us from conventional, average feelings. This, together with his own frequent playing in his perfect and powerful way, could not but be deeply impressive and inspiring to all of us."

As Marta Weigert confirmed, "Busoni never forced his opinion on his pupils. On the contrary, sometimes when he talked about the most important problems, it seemed as if he had not the slightest interest whether we followed and agreed with him. He liked to give himself completely and whoever had open ears could take from him as much as he wanted and had the capacity to take. For many of us, a seed had been planted which was to grow through the years, even throughout a lifetime."

Petri, too, never forced his ideas on his pupils. He suggested, provoked, cajoled. As he often said, "Don't believe anything I tell you. You must convince yourself."

Petri told a story of Busoni as a young man, judging final examinations at the Bologna Conservatory in 1913. He was considering whether or not to pass a student, whereas the administrators and faculty were ready to give full marks. When asked why he was considering failing the student, Busoni proclaimed, "If I myself were to take this examination, I could not give myself more than 50%." Busoni once told Petri that if one is 50% satisfied, one has a right to go on. If not, one should give up. And if one is 80% or more satisfied, one has become deluded.

Petri also related that Busoni, while a judge in a competition, flunked a most gifted, promising candidate. Asked why, Busoni replied, "Too sensitive! He will never survive."

It has already been related how, during Martha Weigert's audition, Busoni illustrated passages from Chopin's G Minor Ballade (see chapter 2, "Influences.") Petri, too, regularly illustrated passages or sections of compositions during sessions with pupils. I recall a private lesson dealing with the sequence of fierce rapid octave passages in the Tchaikovsky Concerto in B-flat, movement one. Petri advised holding the entire lengthy sequence of octaves in a single unified mental image, then performing the octaves rapidly by condensing the image, all the while "shaking the octaves out of one's sleeve" (as Liszt is reported to have done). Petri considered it a grave error to use arm-octaves (rather than wrist/hand octaves), for arm-octaves would hold back the tempo, knot the muscles, and possibly force injury through protracted practice. Suddenly, Petri, in mid-discussion, sitting at his second piano, played the octave passages, in tempo, boldly, forte, voicing the soprano pitch of each octave in turn, never striking the first octave of each sub-phrase the loudest. When finished, he turned back, smiling, and said, "Ah, Alfred, of course, I am an old wreck now. But you can tell from the ruins that I was once a quite respectable building." Though Petri was then in his seventies, no ruins were in evidence, only an older "building." Meanwhile, he had showed me so much more of what I needed to know.[23]

---

[23] See Petri's admirably nuanced Tchaikovsky Concerto recording with the London Symphony under Walter Goer.

And so, we must consider Busoni and Petri as great teachers, no matter their differences. It becomes clear, too, that despite divergent styles of teaching, both artists agreed upon many larger matters dealing with artistry, and teaching such artistry. For example, the need for comprehensive knowledge, deep background, unending excellence through beauty, absolute mastery, deference to, reverence for one's truest account of the immortal masters and their greatest masterpieces. Also, independence in artistry and artistic vision; sublimation of one's personality to that of the composer, the ideal of artistic perfection (though perfection is impossible), the poetic through language, form, and meaning. Lastly, understanding, through both clarity and mystery, by portraying the essentially human through the endless blend of tragedy, comedy, irony, and humor.

Each man took a teaching path according to his own destiny. One thinks of Heraclitus's dictum, "Character is destiny." One admires Petri all the more for carving out his own path as a teacher, as well as pianist, amidst such overpowering influences, and an ever-changing musical and pedagogical landscape.

Soon after arriving in Manchester, England, in 1905, Petri came upon Sir Donald Francis Tovey (1875–1940). From then on, he was a champion of Tovey's invaluable editions with their engaging analyses, (e.g., J. S. Bach's Well-Tempered Clavier, 2 vols.; Beethoven's complete sonatas, 2 vols.; and the Beethoven Essays), unique and deeply informative. When they met in Oxford, Petri related, "I played to him, and he played some Scarlatti. . . . And Tovey said, 'Tell your teacher Busoni not to add octaves to this second voice.'" Ever after, as Egon said, "I have pioneered Tovey in this country [USA] and the Bay Area [CA]. I always use Tovey's Bach exclusively, and I've learned an enormous amount from it." He recounted that Tovey was a delightful, charming personage.[24]

Petri considered one book on piano pedagogy especially worthy: Otto Ortmann's *The Physiological Mechanics of Piano Technique*. He considered the photos alone invaluable (photos tracing actual movements). Ortmann, too, documents the huge variations in body types, and provides exhaustive explications of the body's skeleton, joints, muscles, tendons, etc., and their possible range of movements (all based on Grey's *Anatomy*). How sad that Ortmann's seminal book was published in 1929, when the furor over the economic "crash" buried acknowledgement of this epochal study. How felicitous that Petri was asked—and wrote—a brief forward to this indispensable book! Petri knew Ortmann personally, having dined and conversed with him in Baltimore, where Petri performed several times.

Petri's teaching began and ended with pragmatism. (Pragmatism is defined by *Webster's Dictionary* as "a practical approach, whereby truth is preeminently to be tested by the practical consequences of belief.") Here are more of Petri's remarks as we recorded them:

> "What you create in your piano playing should be least physically taxing, involving the least effort, for the greatest practicable results."
>
> "Be as comfortable as possible, use the ordinary movements of life as much as possible."
>
> "It's no use practicing anything that will never happen."

---

[24] Tovey was also a great pianist. In Aspen, Colorado, Mrs. K. and I heard recordings of Tovey's playing, and remember the interpretations so close to Schnabel's sound and psychological effects. Tovey's comments came from sensibilities gathered from profound artistry plus acute scholarship, a combination most rare. Mrs. K. and I have revered Tovey lifelong, as well. In our teaching, we have continued to use the Tovey editions. And in turn, *our* pupils use the editions if they are teaching!

"First think, then play."

"Practice at last, not at first."

"It is bad to make a general rule."

"Bend the rules to suit the pupil."

"Most difficulties are of your own choosing."

"Once you figure out what's wrong, there are no difficulties."

"Teach the individual only."

"Don't imitate. Be yourself. You will be original because you are yourself and you see with different eyes." "*Quando duo facent, dem non es idem.*" ("When two people do the same thing, it is not the same thing.")

"You must criticize yourself. "

"Once after a concert, a man said to me, 'Maestro, you play wonderfully the study in revolution by Chopin. . . . but, much too fast.' This was such a fearful mixture of a compliment and a criticism all at once. And he was right!"

"There are certain passages that are so quick that they have to be played brilliantly, but I always think of making the piano sing."

Of baroque music: "Well, I try not to make the piano sound like a typewriter. I think I play much more melodiously now than I did when I was young."

"All Mozart's works are operas in disguise."

"Of the composers with true gifts of musical development (Bach, Haydn, Beethoven, Brahms), these are the people who feel well in battle."

"Pull the shade down, don't let in too much sunlight" (concerning a Chopin nocturne).

"The polonaise is not a dance. . . . It is very solemn. The polonaise is a march. Very maestoso and majestic. But it isn't a dance at all."

"It's too musical!" (he complained of certain students).

"I think a pianist should be able to play everything."

"I don't think my playing has ever been dull or metronomic or inexpressive."

"I never play anything without rhythmic consciousness."

"I say there are no bar lines in music."

Of rubato: "I think there is no music that has no rubato."

"I feel in my study of Chopin that he is very much interested in changing rhythmical patterns, not so much the notes, and that certain things have to be played in very strict tempo."

Of rotation, forearm tremulo: "In technique, try to find an example in life where you do a thing like this—a screwdriver, a door knob, or shaking your hand dry. . . . Your body can teach you."

"Mistakes are necessary for progress. You find fingerings out by the mistakes."

"For me, music is a thing that moves me to tears, and expresses emotions as it does in *Don Giovanni*."

"Bach certainly always—or almost always—expresses religious feelings."

"All music is an expression of human sentiment and moods."

"Always think of making the piano sing."

"My heart is in the last century."

"To keep a rigid octave hand position is perfectly wrong."

"You see, the difference between Beethoven and you and me is not that he had more fingers or that his fingers were more agile, but it was his musical imagination."

"The audience doesn't care how hard you work, they just want to hear something."

"Now today [1960s] of course, they [critics, scholars] are so sick of all this romantic business that they call all sentiment and emotion in music romantic. . . . Music is not classic or romantic. . . . All music is romantic, and all music is an expression of human moods. . . . It is coming from the heart and the body and from the basic human psyche. For me there is only one music, and then there are degrees."

"It is not so much the practicing of technique which is important, but the technique of practicing" (a quote of Liszt).

"Don't believe anything I tell you but try it out."

"I think great music is greater than any single performance."

"Nothing can equal independent experimentation."

To be able to master something technically meant for Petri to be able to do one's best musically. In his scores, one regularly saw Petri's various fingerings in rows above especially difficult or formidable passages. His choices were sometimes surprising: a more difficult or most difficult fingering might give the best musical result. In fact, he lived in a realm of musical meanings, and when he had to shift from the endless matters of interpretation to temporarily work on technique alone, he would say, "Pardon me, Mrs. Musick, would you mind just waiting for me? I am coming back to you in a moment."

The idea of using any major portion of time for technique alone was foreign to him. For Petri, "the first rule of music is that music rules."

Regarding specific literature, Petri required the best "unedited" (urtext) editions, with comparisons to autographs, other editions, editors (which Petri sometimes called "additors"). He always kept up with the latest scholarship. For J. S. Bach studies, he soon left Busoni in favor of Tovey. His recognition of the Badura-Skodas soon followed (with Schweitzer ever close behind.)

His ideas of Scarlatti were dutifully accepted from Ralph Kirkpatrick. Beethoven investigations soon superseded von Bülow and Schnabel, proceeded through Tovey (a lifetime favorite), continued through the Henle series, to replicas of manuscripts and autographs, whenever available.

The printed musical page was indelible for Petri. He recalled how a later more accurate edition might upset him during a memorized performance by requiring a different mental page turn! In examining scores, Petri's curiosity was irrepressible, and his delight over what might be found or veiled or hidden ever a cause for excitement. Thinking back, he was everlastingly—curious!

In his autobiography, *Journey of an American Pianist* (2007), Grant Johannesen recalled being sent by his teacher Robert Casadesus to study one summer with Egon Petri, during Petri's early tenure at Cornell University (1940–1947). As he relates:

> Petri had a fanciful way of laying out various editions of Beethoven or Schumann on the floor and then would point at them with a yardstick, before sitting down at the piano to astonish me with his masterful erudition as he "poked and played" his way through combinations of ideas and fingerings. (Incidentally, I was surprised that with this "Bach specialist" there were never any Bach scores in evidence.) Each day, we played scores with only the occasional interruption of his sociable and delightful wife, who would bring coffee and *schlagobers* (whipped cream) for us and usually laughingly comment on the scattered pages of different Beethoven editions on the floor. One of Petri's colleagues at the university, Vladimir Nabokov, the writer, stopped by one day and listened as I played. (pp. 24–25)

As Johannesen summarized, "I had the full attention of a master pianist. I recall my time with Egon Petri fondly. I benefited greatly from his wisdom."

Later in his autobiography, Johannesen added: " . . . under the guidance of great artists like Casadesus and Petri, I was led to a fuller understanding of the music without my mentors trying to tell me what was right or wrong" (p 156). A statement ever susceptible to the deepest consideration.

Petri felt score-marks take much meaning from their setting, that most marks are incomplete (Beethoven's late marks less so), and that nothing is sure. "But there are certain things of which we will never be sure. I think history tells us that," Petri surmised. By endless pragmatism, one must test everything, not only by intuition, but also by evidence. Evidence might be a new, more accurate edition or fresh, more accurate historical sources, or testing different ideas to decide which seem more true to the composer's intention. One's judgment must also come from experience, then, as well as knowledge, the whole through one's expanding understanding.

Jerry Brown, the pragmatic, philosophical governor of California, has said that "one begins by imagining that experience is the problem, but later, one comes to the realization that there is no substitute for experience" (PBS television interview). To repeat, all Petri's solutions, no matter how conditional, were predicated upon experience. Everything was examined, re-examined, tested, even by time. Yet, each solution was provisional, able to be superseded as soon as a better answer appeared, or threatened to emerge. This is close to the scientific method, in a way, calculated to keep one irrevocably in the grips of reality, from which insight can best suggest itself. Meanwhile, absolute concentration was among the first requirements, and for Petri, also among the last.

Petri taught throughout a long, eventful life, with teaching engagements at the Royal College of Music in Manchester, England; the Hochschule für Musik in Berlin; in Basel, Switzerland, and Zakopane, Poland; and later at the Malkin Conservatory in Boston, Cornell University in New York, Mills College in Oakland, California, and the San Francisco Conservatory.

Some of Petri's famous pupils included Earl Wilde, John Ogden, Ruth Slenzynska, Ozan Marsh, Grant Johannesen, Gunner Johansen, Eugene Istomin, Vitya Vronsky (of Vronsky and Babin, duo-pianists), Ernst Levy, Alexander Zakin (Isaac Stern's accompanist for thirty-three years, originally trained at the Berlin Hochschule), Erica Morales, even Victor Borge (popular comedian-musician). Petri received pupils from other master-teachers, such as Busoni, Artur Rubinstein, Robert Casadesus,[25] and Isabella Vengerova.[26] The latter sent pupils to him already while in Berlin ("in the old days"), and later in America. It was about 1911 that Busoni began referring all his pupils to Petri. Other teachers sent him pupils, and pupils sent pupils. (I was first a pupil of a pupil, Professor Henry Gibson of Heidelberg University.)

Still, it was by his many other dedicated students (also Mrs. K. and I) that his influence spread widely in the United States, as well as

---

[25] Robert Casadesus (1899–1972), eminent French pianist and composer. Born in Paris, a scion of a remarkable musical family, he was trained at home and at the Paris Conservatory, where he studied with Louis Diémer and Lucien Capet. Beginning in 1922, he toured widely in Europe. During World War II, he came to the United States, where he performed regularly and taught classes at various schools. After World War II, he taught at the American Conservatory at Fountainebleau. His wife Gaby was also a noted pianist; their son, Jean, was a professional pianist as well. A prolific composer, Robert wrote seven symphonies, a two-piano concerto for himself and Gaby, and a three-piano concerto for Robert, Gaby, and Jean. He was especially renowned for his interpretations of Mozart and the French Impressionists.

[26] Isabelle Vengerova (1877–1956), distinguished Russian pianist and pedagogue. A pupil of Anna Essipoff and Theodore Leschetizky, she received a teaching appointment at the St. Petersburg Conservatory in 1906 and toured Russia until the revolution. She toured the United States in 1923, becoming a professor at the Curtis Institute of Music in Philadelphia upon its founding in 1924. She taught privately in New York as well. An internationally recognized pedagogue, some of her famous pupils at Curtis were Leonard Bernstein, Samuel Barber, Lukas Foss, and Gary Graffman. Nicholas Slonimsky was her famous, singular nephew.

in Europe and Australia. And here, now, perhaps he will also inspire you, Dear Reader. Petri's recordings are still treasured, and his teaching ideals still being tested and successfully applied. He might be surprised at this, though we are not.

Of teaching and performing, Petri once said he was "caught between the two stools of teaching and playing, which is not a good idea." He thought "the best pianists don't teach." Nevertheless, lifelong, Petri performed *and* taught. "I was a rather good teacher, and other people thought so too."

But, in times of crisis, as when a world war intervenes, pupils can evaporate. As Petri recounted, "When the War broke out in 1914, I was then in St. Petersburg [Petri's first visit to Russia, then still under the Czar]. I remember meeting d'Albert at the Hotel Astoria and we had a little lunch together." Petri had seen the Cherkassian regiments drilling, "and I thought, what are they doing here?" Back in Berlin, almost all Petri's pupils left, since most were foreigners, Italian, English, Americans, Russians. As he said, "I only had one pupil left, who gave me forty marks" (a large fee).

"In Berlin we lived in a flat during the War [World War I]. And we were really hungry. We had to go out, and we had ration cards for everything. . . . We got, I believe, one herring a week, and bread was made of sawdust. Hardly any flour in it. As marmalade we had turnips. No coffee." (For their safety, the Petris had sent their three children to Holland.) "We stayed in Berlin three years, from 1914 to 1917. Three miserable years! I had no good pupils anymore. I had two or three German pupils. . . . That's all. And occasional small concerts in Germany."

However, there was one Polish pupil who, seeing the Petri family in dire circumstances, arranged through a friend for Petri to give a concert in Zakopane, Poland. "There, I stayed in a boarding house, and met some wonderful people who were very hospitable and warm-hearted and faithful. In Zakopane, people embraced me and would say tearfully,

'*Es war wunderbar*! ('It was wonderful!') And this went on. . . . Soon I began to play in Krakow, Lodz, Warsaw. I was quite successful everywhere in Poland. This was still during the War in 1917. . . .

"I used to go in trains where all the windows were broken . . . and it being winter, it was so cold that I had to wrap myself in a big rug and a fur coat so that my nose alone was showing out. . . . What saved me was my Dutch passport." (In 1917–1918, the Germans occupied Warsaw.)

"Soon I was making money on my concerts, and I had pupils in all these (Polish) towns. . . . Once in Krakow, I was not paid in money, but in flour. I had to carry it over my shoulder to my hotel. That was my fee." Another time, "I was given a whole box of eggs. At that time, we ate about one egg a week. Well, I brought these things back to Berlin with me, and I was a savior."

Finally, in 1917, the Petris moved to Poland, remaining there until 1921. So, for the Petris, pupils and performances remained mutually nourishing. Many Poles became close friends, including the director of the Zakopane Sanitarium, whose wife was the sister of Madame Curie. "She became our greatest friend," recalled Petri. In acknowledgement of such kindnesses and friendships, Petri said he once played Liszt's arrangement of Beethoven's 9th Symphony for the Sanatorium audience. (Over the years, Petri gave at least fifty recitals there.)

After some years in Berlin, as professor at the Hochschule für Musick, 1921–1926, Petri and his family moved back to Poland in 1927, maintaining his headquarters there until 1939, occasionally returning to Berlin, when the Second World War intervened! The Petris fled Zakopane the day before the Nazi invasion of Poland (again!), abandoning his library of rare editions, manuscripts, and three hundred letters of Busoni.[27]

---

[27] When Hitler came to power, Petri severed all ties to the Berlin Hochschule as a little-publicized protest against the persecution of his Jew-

In Utrecht, Holland, on 17 October 1939, Petri wrote a letter informing EMI of his whereabouts:

> We left Zakopane on Aug 25th—just in time—and I have been sitting around here waiting for a boat to take us to America. . . . I have probably lost all my belongings in Poland (there is absolutely no news—terrible. Poor, poor Poland!) & certainly, all my concerts in England so far. Today I should have played in Zurich, but as I did not know when we should be able to sail I had to cancel it... Fortunately I had enough funds to tide me over these 2 months here and if I get safely to America I shall be all right—at least financially.[28]
>
> We shall sail this Saturday. Let us hope there won't be any torpedoes or mines.

Again, Petri had lost all his pupils and his concerts. Fortunately, there were no torpedoes or mines. He would soon be saved by teaching posts at the Malkin Conservatory in Boston, and Cornell University in Ithaca, New York. Again, performing gained him admirers and pupils. His weekly Sunday radio broadcasts from Cornell certainly helped, at the outset. It was by then obvious that Petri enjoyed teaching, and was therein completely absorbed. He felt gratified helping students, thus advancing his beloved art through instructing as well as performing. It was already evident, too, that although the statement "the best pianists don't teach" is true, it is also untrue. Teaching and performing can be two noble facets ("caught between two stools") of one career!

---

ish colleagues. As he said, "For me, it was easy. . . . I left in 1933, because I saw the uprising under Hitler (I was almost beaten by one of those SS men in Dresden) and I thought that this is nothing for me and I stood up for my Jewish colleagues. . . . I'm glad I did it, although Mrs. Busoni and my wife both advised me to play in Germany. I said I will not do it because I played with Bruno Walter, Klemperer, made records with Szigeti, who were now forbidden in Germany." Petri never performed in Germany again.

[28] As reproduced in the program notes for APR recording 7701.

Before I close here, a vital aspect of Petri's teaching must be emphasized: besides his ability to fasten on the smallest or largest technical problem and solve it, to reapply the most appropriate musical sensibilities, he made sure that an embracing emotional/psychological/historical picture would be placed before each student. Petri might question a single word, and alter one's conception of it: "What I call 'practicing' is not what most persons call practicing. . . . I played this [Brahms B-flat concerto] in public, but I never finished practicing it." Elaborating further, "I 'practiced' in the sense that I committed all these pieces to memory and thought about them and didn't stop until I could do what I thought the composer meant."

Sometimes a few words would suffice: "Listen to Mozart's operas and string quartets, not other pianists." Or, by diversion, in the midst of a technical discussion with Mrs. K., a few kind words: "Why didn't you inform your mother before you were born that you want to be a concert pianist, so she could have arranged for nice large hands. . . . You have everything else."

Other times, a lengthier account would be necessary:

There was the American Quartet at the time that Brahms was still alive. I don't know whether it is true or not, but still, the story has a germ of truth. They had played the Brahms quartets and loved them very much, and they toured in America. They played them at a certain tempo, and Brahms was still alive. The first violinist said, "You know, we have an engagement in Germany, in Austria, and I will write Brahms and ask him if he would be gracious enough to listen to our playing and tell us his opinion of his quartets." Brahms wrote a very nice letter back, "I will be very pleased to listen to you at such and such a time, in my rooms." Then the first violinist said, "I know Brahms, and I know he likes very slow tempos, so let's slow our tempos to about half of what we have been playing in America!" They had quite a bit of trouble holding back, but they got used to it, and were able to do it at a reduced speed. And then they came to Brahms. After they had finished playing, Brahms said, "Bravissimo, bravissimo, Gentlemen . . . but please, why so quick?"

Other times, only a protracted soliloquy would suffice, as when Petri related the following to Mrs. K. and me after hearing a gifted pupil perform the Schumann Fantasie:

It was brilliant and much too quick, not enough poetic manner . . . too contemporary, looking out for speed, etc. If [this pupil] had not been born in this country [USA], it would be the best thing. But to be born in Germany at the time I was when Clara Schumann and the tradition were still alive and in the air. . . . But [this pupil] has to learn this. A fish born in the water doesn't have to learn swimming. I was first in Leipzig where Mendelssohn revived Bach—Mendelssohn conducted there—and then in Dresden when I was eight, Carl Weber conducted Wagner, and where Strauss had his first performance. Anyhow, I lived in an atmosphere and read all the contemporary romantics—Hoffmann, Jean Paul (Richter), Novalis and all these romantic poets. I was familiar with them. Schumann was influenced by all these. The Kreisleriana was taken from Hoffmann's autobiography . . . the motto of the Schumann Fantasie is "through all dreams on earth there is one soft tone which is audible to him who seeketh and listens." If you don't know the spirit and literature of that age, how can you understand Schumann, who was so much a part of it?[29]

---

[29] Petri felicitously quotes Friederich Schlegel's motto, which Schumann originally affixed to his great Fantasie, Op. 17:

Durch Alle Töne tönet
Im bunten Erdentraum
Ein Leiser Ton gezogen
Für den der Heimlich lauschet. (See translation on following page.)

I think if this student read these things now she would probably say "Throw this book away—I can't read anything so old fashioned." You have to live in that atmosphere. If you can't play the music of the composer without knowing everything about him and his times, you simply aren't a good musician. It may not be that you play the

---

Through all the tones of earth's
So multicolored dream
One muted tone is drawn
For one who secretly listens. (trans. A. Kanwischer)

In his daybook (*Tagebucher* 1827–1838), Schumann wrote to Clara Wieck, "The 'Tone' in the motto is you, isn't that so?" (quoted in Peter Ostwald, *Schumann*, 1985, p. 127). This seems not only fresh confirmation of Robert's true affection for Clara during their long separation, but also clear acknowledgement of his deepest admiration for her superb artistry. Similarly, regarding the "Tone," Ferruccio Busoni, rather than believing in many, or innumerable kinds of music, took the view that but a single music exists as an ideal, of which classic masterpieces are merely imperfect fragments (Dent, 1933, p. 306). Busoni imagined that a great artist could immerse himself in the great mystery of that Ideal, in a kind of music into which one might melt or dissolve ("auflössen"). Egon Petri, too, said something similar: "For me, there is only one music, and then there are degrees" (as quoted above, this chapter). Schumann's music meanwhile, has never been easily understood. After Robert's death, Liszt regretted that, despite his determined, even Byronic, advocacy, "The public has no taste (for Schumann's piano pieces) and most pianists didn't understand him" (quoted in G. Eisman, *Robert Schumann*, 1956, vol. 1, p. 128). Clara, too, repeatedly urged Robert to write music more accessible to general audiences. (The piano concerto ended in being one such.) One hopes, in the twenty-first century of computers, there will still be those rare great interpreters and listeners of Schumann's masterpieces, for, as Petri says so well, Schumann's music will ever demand grave understanding and empathy for Robert's and Clara's world, and Schlegel's secret "Tone."

J.S. Bach's ThomasSchule in Leipzig as sketched in watercolors by Felix Mendelssohn. The view is from the house in which Mendelssohn lived in 1839 and 1842. Lbrecht Music and Arts / Alamy Stock Photo.

music better, but that you get greater enjoyment out of it. . . . I can't judge myself, because I was born in those times of the Schumann Fantasie. I even met Mme. Schumann when I was five years old. I lived in that atmosphere when all this happened, and therefore I have a better key to all these things than an American [pupil] who is interested in winning a contest . . . and interested primarily in Accuracy, Speed, and Power, the new trinity! And then the music comes later, or it doesn't come at all.

Then, as if answering himself, Petri said:

Of course, if you are not a musician, then this information doesn't help you at all. You can't play the "Appassionata" Sonata by reading biographic materials about Beethoven and his times. . . . But, (if you are a musician), it most certainly helps to know something about the times of the composer.

Asked why he had never written a book on teaching, Petri replied, "It is my conviction that it is better to work in living material and teach young students than to write books about it, especially as I am not a literary man." In the *Saturday Review*, Jan Holcman confirmed: "Petri was true to himself and conscious of the missionary aspects of a great interpreter."

Despite Petri's constant cheerfulness, his reverence for the greatest art remained immutable, sacrosanct. He always continued probing—all was fluid. He considered learning endless, necessary, salutary. For Petri, teaching was an exercise in hope, a service, a benefit, a gift. His example can serve for a lifetime.

Chapter 4
Repertoire and Performance

I am here to defend the composer.

Egon Petri

Petri's encyclopaedic knowledge of the piano literature and
his colossal performing repertoire . . .

Bryan Crimp 1994

Petri's repertoire was enormous, taking in most of Beethoven,
Liszt, Chopin, Schumann, Brahms, and fair amounts of Bach,
Schubert, Mozart, and Mendelssohn. A typical program in New York
City described by Philip Moores: 33 Diabelli Variations of Beethoven, 12 Alkan Etudes, and 12 Chopin Etudes, Op. 10. Glazunov
(quoted in Shostakovich's *Testimony*) describes a Petri recital in Russia, an all-Liszt program consisting of the "Don Juan" Fantasy, the B
Minor Sonata, and the "Dante" Sonata. Glazunov described it as "a
champion performance."

As well, in his early years, Petri performed "modern" music, in-
cluding involvement in the first Berlin performance of Schönberg's
Pierrot Lunaire, and considerable amounts of Alkan (preludes, etudes,
the Piano Symphony, arranged from Etudes Op. 39, 4–7), also
Medtner, Griffes, Casella, and Busoni. The Russians, Stravinsky
(Petruschka Suite), Prokofieff (Sonata No. 3 and Toccata), Glazunov,
Rachmaninoff (including both suites for two pianos), and Scriabin
(Sonata No. 4 and etudes), appeared on his recital programs in Russia.

Petri gave Mrs. K. and me two catalogues of his repertoire (mentioned in the Preface; see Appendix). The wide range of literature and length of the programs are startling. He seemed fearless; for example, in Dublin in 1931 (at age fifty), two recitals in one day: in the afternoon, Bach's Goldberg Variations and Beethoven's "Hammerclavier" Sonata; in the evening, Beethoven's "Waldstein" Sonata and Liszt's six "Paganini" Etudes. His recital at the Meister Saal in Berlin on 7 June 1932 seems a pinnacle: Bach-Busoni Toccata in D minor, two chorale-preludes, the "St. Anne" Prelude and Fugue, Franck's Prelude, Chorale and Fugue, Brahms' "Paganini" Variations,[30] Schubert-Liszt 6 Lieder, and Liszt's Don Juan Fantasie.

In his first American tour in 1932, Petri appeared three times in Town Hall in New York City in the space of four months, besides appearing with an orchestra at Carnegie Hall and the Metropolitan Opera House.

Again, in New York City in 1933–1934, during one month, he performed six different concertos with the NBC Orchestra (including Mozart, Beethoven's "Emperor," Liszt, and Tchaikovsky). Mean-

---

[30] Petri is widely admired for his recording of the Brahms-Paganini Variations. In talk among pianists as diverse as Garrick Ohlsson and Jean Phillip Collard, once Petri was mentioned, each soon exclaimed, "Ah, the Brahms-Paganini!" "And, so musical!" Within the invaluable APR reissue (APR 7701) of the complete Columbia and Electrola recordings of Petri from 1929–1951, one finds Petri performances not only of the Brahms-Paganini Variations, but also the Brahms-Handel Variations, the three Brahms Rhapsodies, the four Ballades Op. 10, and Six Pieces Op. 118. It may surprise some listeners that, although endlessly expressive, Petri keeps his interpretations formally taut, with a marked steadiness of tempo. As he would tell his pupils, "In Brahms, not so much rubato. Brahms was not that kind of man." All told, these performances confirm Petri as a great Brahms interpreter.

while, in Colorado Springs in 1933, Petri gave a masterclass and five recitals in one month. The last recital, on 30 May, consisted of Chopin's Sonata in B-flat, Bach's Goldberg Variations, and Beethoven's Sonata Op. 111.

Portrait from *Egon Petri: The Complete Columbia and Electrola Solo and Concert Recordings 1929–1951*, a CD set issued in 2015 by APR (7701).

Here is a fully loaded first half of a recital in Kingston, England, in 1934: Beethoven's "Appassionata" Sonata and the Brahms Handel Variations. Or this: in Glasgow in 1935, he performed Brahms' gigantic Second Concerto and Liszt's E-flat Concerto. Another peak: in Wigmore Hall, London, in 1935, he played the "Hammerclavier" Sonata and the entirety of Liszt's Second Year of Pilgrimage (Italian). How wonderful it would have been to be there! Only the next year, in London, 1936, within three programs over three days, he traversed the entire Liszt's Transcendental Etudes.

The most remarkable aspect of this phenomenon was not the enormity of the programs, but the standard of excellence he maintained. His conviction was that one must be ready to do one's best at the outset. Even in his recording sessions, he never re-recorded or spliced. What you hear is his first complete performance. Once, just after he had recorded in New York City, he told my wife and me, "It was too hot, and I didn't want to weary the technicians, so I just played everything through so that we could all go home."

One evening in his home, Busoni told his guests he had just finished composing his Toccata. He could not play it for them since he was indisposed. Petri said, "Well, let me look at it a while, then, perhaps I can play it through." Petri went into an adjoining room for about forty-five minutes. Only near the end did the guests hear a phrase or two of music, played softly, slowly, deliberately. Then Petri returned, and played the Toccata through. Toward its end Busoni whispered, "He can do these things better than I." (In New York, Busoni once told the pianist and composer Phillip Jarnach the same thing.)[31]

It was known that Petri spent most of his rehearsal time studying the music. Even if time were short, most of it would be spent examining the score, before turning to the keyboard.

Petri was known as a superb Liszt player. Even early, he related, "Once I played some Liszt under him [Sir Henry Wood] in London. He stopped the orchestra during a rehearsal and said, 'This is how Liszt ought to be played.'"

Late in his life, Petri performed Busoni's monumental Fantasia contrapuntistica once more, in the two-piano version on KPFA Radio, Berkeley, California (where my wife and I and others also gave live

---

[31] In listening to Petri's performances of Busoni's compositions on APR 7701, one is struck by his sympathetic understanding of each idiosyncratic unfolding. One can imagine Busoni coming to such a conclusion.

studio recitals), this time with the distinguished Italian pianist, Carlo Busotti. Afterwards I asked "How did it feel?" "It was lovely," Egon replied. "It was just like performing with myself." So, we see that Petri had long before left the shadow of Busoni, and had become a confident, wholly independent musician. (And it was a grand compliment to Busotti, surely.)

Of Petri's appointment to Mills College in California in the 1950s, Petri's pupil Grant Johannesen wrote in his autobiography,

> I have admiration for people who, after they have achieved success in something, dare to explore new frontiers. There [in California] he played the Fauré quartets with the Pro Arte Quartet, which was in residence. Milhaud headed up the music department at the time. They all became great friends, and Petri actually played the first performance of Milhaud's Piano Quintet, which is not an easy piece. Frankly, I can't imagine him playing it, but apparently at Mills College he became fascinated with a lot of repertoire he hadn't known before—a good example of a musically curious, though elderly pianist. (*Journey of an American Pianist*, p. 175)

About Petri's great affinity for Beethoven: in 1959, at the San Francisco Museum of Art, he performed all thirty-two sonatas in a series of six concerts. When he played the opening movement of the "Moonlight" Sonata, veiled, ghostly, harp-like sonorities emerged, seemingly from another world, whereby it seemed as if he kept the damper pedal depressed for the whole movement (as Beethoven notates in his score). It was uncanny, the audience transfixed—and this on a newer American Steinway.

Years later, in 1968 Mrs. K. and I were powerfully reminded of this during our visit to the Kunsthistorisches Museum in Vienna, where we played on Beethoven's own original pianos, the Erard grand of 1803 and the Broadwood of 1807. When Mrs. K. played the opening movement of the "Moonlight" on those pianos, we realized with a start that Egon, back in 1959, had so closely approximated those ethereal, ghostly, harp-like sonorities.

It was only later I realized that Egon in his youth would have heard pianos thirty or forty years old, which would place them around 1850–1870, so much closer to the sound-effects of Beethoven's Erard and Broadwood. Yet, it took Egon's seminal imagination to make such a complete connection in Beethoven's "Moonlight" Sonata. (Incidentally, this late performance in 1959 was quite different from Petri's earlier recording in 1937.)

Limited space forbids discussion of a host of other attributes of early pianos as documented in Beethoven's piano sonatas, such as orchestral string choirs, string quartet writing, solo string writing, orchestral tuttis, horn calls, concerto discourse, cadenzas, vocal writing (aria, song, chorale, recitative), organ textures, counterpoint, pedal-points, dance-drones, etc. When Egon performed Beethoven sonatas, the listener could discern that such multifarious references were being assimilated and portrayed.

Of course, more recent and contemporary pianos can infer many of Beethoven's references, if the pianist is aware of them and makes the necessary adjustment of touch, articulation, voicing, and pedaling effects. Then, too, modern pianos can do things that earlier pianos could not, or could only suggest, such as more plangent tone colors, more sustaining of tones, more power, objectives toward which the ideal piano in Beethoven's inner ear was pointing in his final years. Egon said, "You can re-create historic performance ideals, but you can't re-create the audience."

This proves once again that, as Petri directed, we must look back continually, thoughtfully, to former times—to history—and also look forward beyond the present, to bring the full measure of meaning to the timeless messages of great music. "Each performance is only an interpretation," as Egon said. (And, one hopes, a reinterpretation.) In looking back, it would seem that Egon had an easier time in the twentieth century comprehending the nineteenth-century music world than we do in the twenty-first. As Petri said to us more than once, "My heart is in the last century." (Wagner died when Egon was two, Liszt died when Egon was five; Tchaikovsky died when Egon was twelve; Clara Schuman died when Egon was fifteen; Brahms died when Egon was sixteen; and Mahler died when Egon was thirty.) Petri was for us an historical human bridge. It was exhilarating to witness and enter his world. We still treasure the times.

Even lately, Mrs. K. and I have spoken to elderly people who heard Petri's weekly radio broadcasts from Cornell University, which covered so much diverse literature. A newspaper report says that these broadcasts reached millions. He gave a similar series in Basel, Switzerland, in the years 1959–1960, some portions of which were subsequently offered as recordings. In Egon's occasional radio broadcasts at KPFA in Berkeley, California, he usually gave a series of three recitals. One program could hardly suffice to open the gates to Petri's vast landscape of piano literature. Yet, in each concert, the listener, rather than hear an evening of music, could enter Petri's world of sensibilities and references, meanings—embracing, historical, timeless.

In asking Egon questions, which I recorded on the tapes mentioned in the Preface, he responded with manifold answers both personal and unitary.

I asked, "In performing, some people ask, 'Do you think of the composer first, the performer, the audience, the instrument, or the music first?'" Egon answered:

> He [the performer] should certainly not think of himself. He should certainly not think of his audience, because if he plays beautifully, the audience will be delighted. Not because he wants to delight the audience, but because he plays so beautifully that the audience can't help liking it, you see. . . . You should think about the music first. You should imagine the music and you should hear it before you ev-

er go to a piano. . . . He must know his piano. If he doesn't know his piano then he won't know how to do it. He should not think of himself. Forget himself as much as possible. He can't help being himself. . . . If I play a Beethoven sonata and then Gould plays it and then Richter plays it and so on, there may be dissimilarities, but the similarities are much greater. And I don't think of me and say, 'Oh, look at me, how I play the piano.' And if I detect a little germ of this, I sort of say, 'Now, go away!' I don't encourage it, you see. Of course, I am vain like everyone else, and I like to be praised and loved rather than hated. . . . People have said to me, 'Your playing is divine.' And I say, 'Listen here, reserve that term for Mozart and Haydn and all these people. But I am only a recreator. I know perfectly well that I haven't made the sun and the moon, or the birds and the flowers.

Question: "Is there any inherent conflict between trying to create 'perfect' performances technically and/or artistically and aesthetically?" Egon replied, "No, there shouldn't be. It should all be one. It should be like an embryo that is all complete in itself and then just develops. You can take a rose. . . . It is all contained in the seed. So, you should never play anything with attention to only one point (not like the pupil who once said to me, 'Oh, I haven't put the expression in yet.'). You should always think of making beautiful music."

Another question: "There seems to be a problem with many pupils and performers that the music, when it becomes intense, creates a tension within them." Egon: "Well, you see, these are the amateurs. They become so involved in the emotion of the music that they are all tense. He is not above his work, but is drowning in his work. You must try to eliminate every unnecessary effort." This again reflects Egon's determination to rise *above* all obstacles, to best command all one's resources.

Then I asked, "And what of performers' extreme gestures?" Egon: "As soon as it [a gesture] hinders you technically, then it becomes a detriment. . . . I make a great distinction between necessary movements . . . and other things which are dramatic gestures. Gestures are not necessary, but they are also not forbidden. . . . When gestures become mannerisms. . . . For instance, I have seen a famous pianist nearly fall over at the end of the E-flat major Concerto of Beethoven. I am sure they (such performers) don't use these extreme gestures when they are recording . . . and they certainly don't use them when they are engaged to play very, very quickly."

Question: Do you believe these mannerisms are sincere? Egon: "I don't think they can be."

Regarding that illusory and chimerical thing called "perfection" in performance, Egon offered,

> Of course, there is always something that miscarries in a performance. I don't think any good pianist, real artist, has ever been satisfied with his performance and can say, "Well, this is exactly what I wanted to do." We all have an ideal in our head, I hope, and it is so wonderful what we think, what the music ought to sound like, you see, and we compare it to what we play, to the ideal. Of course, the audience is unable to hear this. They can't know what I intended to do. And for me it can be a great disappointment, and I say "Oh, that wasn't at all what I wanted to do." And they say, "Oh, but it was marvellous, wonderful" because they hear the actual things and cannot compare it with the ideal in your head. . . . You see, Schumann was very wise in this way, he divided himself into three persons: Eusebius was the dreamer, Floristan was the passionate one, and Master Raro, the critic. Well, naturally, while I play, I am listening to myself, and I am criticizing myself. But I can't help that, you see. . . . You *must* criticize yourself, or you go to the dogs![32]

---

[32] Artists don't often articulate this kind of admission, but they live with it perpetually. Recall, Busoni said that if one were 50% happy, one had the right to go on. But, if one were 80% or more satisfied, one had become de-

Egon was not a religious man, but he firmly believed in the healing power of music. (There had been deaths and births during his concerts. For example, as Egon related, in Poland a man had a heart attack during Egon's performance of Chopin's Funeral March. Another time, a woman in his audience had to be removed to the vestibule of a concert hall to give birth.)

Postlude

As related earlier, in the period 1927–1939, Petri and his family made their home in Zakopane, Poland, since the Poles, like the Russians, especially revered Petri's artistry.[33] Zakopane, reminiscent of the Swiss Tyrol, was then Poland's most fashionable mountain resort. At the foot of a mountain, not far from his home, was a TB sanitarium (of which Paderewski was chief stockholder). Petri related that he performed there over fifty times during those years. He would pack his concert clothes in a knapsack, say goodbye to his charming wife,

---

luded. (See chapter 3, "Teaching") After a long lifetime of endless performing, Isaac Stern wrote, "I don't think I've ever felt that I reached the true heart of any work" (*My First 79 Years*, Knopf, 1999, p. 297). The incandescent perfectionist Arturo Toscanini once told another conductor, "I have never had one moment of complete satisfaction" (*Toscanini: An Intimate Portrait*, by Samuel Chotzinoff, Knopf, 1956, p. 75). When Toscanini screamed and raged at his orchestra, "You are nothing, I am nothing, Beethoven is everything!," he meant it absolutely. Beethoven wrote, "The true artist has no pride; unhappily, he realizes that art has no limitations, he feels darkly how far he is from the goal, and while, perhaps, he is admired by others, he grieves that he has not reached the point where the better genius shall shine before him like a distant star" (Teplitz, July 17, a letter to a ten-year-old admirer). Indeed, such admissions, like Egon's, provide solace to all artists who continue lifelong to aspire, despite all human limitations.

[33] In recognition of Petri's lifelong artistry, the Polish government awarded him the medal "Order of Polonia Restituta."

Mitta Schön-Petri, and his three children, Jan, Peter, and Ulla, and ski down the mountain to the sanitarium, his mind and spirit full of the music to be played. On one occasion in 1935, the program was this: Bach-Busoni 4 Chorale Preludes; Beethoven's Sonata Op. 81a; Chopin: Impromptu in F-sharp, Nocturne in B-flat, four Etudes Op. 25, and Scherzo in C-sharp minor; Liszt's Petrarch Sonnet in E Op. 104, Gnomes's Dance, St. Francis Walking on the Water, and Venezia e Napoli (Gondoliera-Canzone-Tarantella)!

Let's leave him there, flying down the mountain, enveloped by such music. It's a lovely image to keep in the near recesses of one's mind while so often facing such a pessimistic, derelict, and dangerous world, an image to keep close, whenever needed!

Postscript

As mentioned in the Preface, all Petri's Columbia and Electrola recordings from 1929 through 1951 have been lovingly remastered in CD format (seven discs) by APR (Appian Publications & Recordings Ltd.), a great achievement and an invaluable gift. Here is Petri's magisterial artistry clearly and finely displayed (APR 7701, 2016).

The excellent and perceptive program notes by Bryan Crimp and Mark Ainley have highly complimentary things to say of Egon's artistry, all fully justified. It's heartening to witness savants of later generations, by now so far removed from his times, recognizing and acknowledging Petri's timeless art.

Jeremy Nicholas's advance review of the APR set (APR 7701) in *Gramophone Magazine* (December 2015) is valuable and revealing. At the outset he states, "You will hear piano playing raised to spectacular and impassioned heights, and a tonal palette that was as varied in its colors as it was subtly and tastefully applied." Later, Nicholas declares, "Time and again it is Petri's astounding technique that causes one to stop in wonder." At the last he justly acknowledges that "Mark Obert-Thorn's audio restoration has achieved remarkably uniform results and APR's annotation and presentation are, as always, the standard for the industry."

Many have said that Petri was at his best in the grand, large, epic pieces. This is true, but it is not the whole truth. It is clear from these collected recordings that Egon had a great flair for portraying shorter works also, even miniatures. (For example, see especially his Schubert-Liszt *Gretchen am Spinnrade*.)

Through these recordings, Petri's very choice of literature and his artistic vision still live. In a single stroke, APR has ensured the survival of Egon's poetic artistry for a new generation, for a new century. We give them grateful thanks. Egon was a guiding light throughout his life; now, through this reissue and others, he belongs to the ages.

Appendix

The following is a list of compositions performed by Egon Petri from 1892 through 1929, in alphabetical order by composer, including location and date of performance. The information was compiled by "F.S." (author unknown) in July of 1933 in Zakopane, Poland. These are performances, then, from Egon's childhood, age eleven, through his forty-eighth year. One supposes this revelatory list was derived from programs and/or other materials available to F.S. in 1933. The Appendix is a replica of a bound booklet given by Egon to Mrs. K and me during our association in California in the 1950s.

There are five subdivisions: (1) violin solo ("Violine," p. 1); (2) chamber music ("Kammermusick," pp. 1–2), wherein Egon was second violinist in his father's string quartet; (3) organ solo ("Orgel," p. 2); (4) piano solo ("Klavier," pp. 2–19); and (5) chamber music ("Kammermusik," pp. 20–24), wherein Egon was chamber pianist. Of the parenthesis under subdivision 5 (p. 20), the translation is this: "with the exception of song accompaniments." This implies that there was in existence a separate list of lieder with Egon as accompanist which was omitted.

However, in all these subdivisions, it is evident that this Appendix is incomplete. For example, Egon mentioned performing organ works other than those listed here (i.e., Bach, Reger, Franck). The extensive piano solo list (subdivision 4) does not include Egon's tours of Russia, beginning in 1923, which probably involved more than three hundred recitals. Then there were his fifty or so recitals at the Sanitarium in Zakopane. Bear in mind, too, that by age fourteen, Egon was engaged as violinist in the Dresden Opera Orchestra, and sometimes played in his father's string quartet in these earlier years.

The great Hungarian violinist Joseph Szigetti, in his program notes for his recording EMI (HQM 1127) related that, since meeting Egon at Busoni's home in 1912, "We [Joseph and Egon] had frequently appeared together, toured the English provinces, played many sonata recitals in Soviet Russia in the late 1920's." These recital programs are not documented here. Szigetti states simply, "My partner on another of these recordings, Egon Petri, is also a personality who belongs to history, as one of the greatest pianists of his time." There are undoubtedly still other of Egon's performances of the period 1892 through 1929 which do not appear here. This Appendix is fulsome, then, but far from complete.

Notice in subdivision 4, Piano Solo, one finds more than twenty concertos, including the Bach Concerto in D Minor (with Busoni as conductor), the Bach C Minor for Two Klavier, five of Beethoven, and those of Brahms, Chopin, Liszt, six of Mozart, Schumann, Saint-Saëns, Tchaikovsky, and Weber. This list is incomplete also.

Sprinkled among the Piano Solo columns are a goodly number of works for two pianos, besides Busoni's Fantasia contrapuntistica (also performed in Wigmore Hall, London, in 1921), for example, Debussy's *En blanc et noir*, Debussy's Three Pieces, Liszt's monumental Concerto Pathétique for Two Pianos (which has been such an imposing factor in the lives of Dr. and Mrs. K.), Mozart-Busoni works for two pianos (see p. 16), Variations of Saint-Saëns, Reger, and especially the two epic Suites, Op. 5 and Op. 17 of Rachmaninoff (also our daunting lifelong companions, as they are for every striving duo-piano team).

In all Egon's adventuring through the literature in his endless touring, there should be an exclamation mark on the last page of this Appendix, where we see he performed Stravinsky's *Pergolese-Suite* in Madrid in 1929. Lovely!

There is in subdivision 4 also an imposing amount of Bach-Busoni (p. 8, sixteen items), Beethoven-Busoni, Brahms-Busoni, and

Liszt-Busoni, as well as Bach Petri (p. 5, nine items). Egon recounted to us that regularly, after a concert, admirers would come up to Busoni and say, "Oh, Mr. Bach-Busoni, it's such a pleasure to meet you." This did not please Busoni.

This Appendix, then, clearly reflects its Time, but it also contains an admirable proportion of immortal masterworks. Lastly, here, I place together five mottos that Egon told to me at various times over the years:

"You must know the music."

"You must know the composer."

"You must know your piano."

"You must know the Times."

"You must know yourself."

And so he did.

That is why we can say, regarding Egon Petri—solo and chamber violinist, solo pianist, organist, chamber musician—in the most salutary way, this repertoire list mirrors the man.

E G O N   P E T R I

R E P E R T O I R E

Das vorliegende Verzeichnis ist nach den Programmen
zusammengestellt und enthält die bis zum Sommer 1931 in
den Konzerten gespielten Werke. Diese sind nach den Namen
der Komponisten alphabetisch geordnet. Ort und Datum be-
ziehen sich auf den ersten öffentlichen Vortrag.

Zakopane, Juli 1933. F. S.

The text on the opening page of the booklet may be translated as follows:

The following inventory is assembled from concert programs of performances until the summer of 1931. This collection is in alphabetical order by composer. The location and date refer to the earliest public performance.

Zakopane, July 1933. F. S.

Violine

Solo

Bériot	Violinkonzert Nr. 7, G-dur, Satz 2 und 1 (mit Klavier, arr.)	Dresden	1894
Nardini	Sonate D-dur, Satz 1 und 2 (mit Klavier)	"	1892
Petri	Romanze (mit Klavier)	"	1894

Kammermusik

(Zweite Violine im Streichquartett des Vaters)

Artschibuschew, Skrjabin, Glasunow, Rimsky-Korssakow, Liadow, Wihtol, Blumenfeld, Ewald, Winkler, Sokolow:	Variationen über ein russisches Volkslied für Streichquartett (mit Henri Petri, Alfred Spitzner und Georg Wille)	Dresden	1900
Beethoven	Streichquartett D-dur op. 18,3 (mit Henri Petri, Bernhard Unkenstein und Georg Wille)	Halle	1899
	Streichquartett Es-dur op. 47 (mit denselben)	"	1900
Brahms	Streichquartett c-moll op. 51,1 (mit denselben)	"	1899
Cherubini	Streichquartett Nr. 1 Es-dur (mit Henri Petri, Alfred Spitzner und Georg Wille)	Dresden	1900
Dittersdorf	Streichquartett Es-dur (mit Henri Petri, Bernhard Unkenstein und Georg Wille)	Halle	1899
Dvořák	Klavierquintett A-dur op. 81 (mit denselben; Klavier: Alexander Siloti)	"	1900
Haydn	Streichquartett Nr. 36 Es-dur (mit Henri Petri, Bernhard Unkenstein und Georg Wille)	"	1900
Schubert	Streichquartett a-moll op. 29 (mit denselben)	"	1900

2

Schumann	Streichquartett a-moll op. 41,1 (mit denselben)	Halle 1900

O r g e l

Busoni-Stock	Fantasia contrappuntistica (unter Oskar Fried)	Berlin 1912
Corelli	Sonate für Violine und Orgel (arr.) (mit Henri Petri)	Dresden 1912
Mozart	Adagio aus dem Violinkonzert A-dur (K.-V. 219) für Violine und Orgel arr. (mit Henri Petri)	" 1912

K l a v i e r

Solo

Alkan

Etude G-dur op. 35,3

Etude d-moll (en rhythme op. 39,2   molossique)

Aus: 48 Motifs, op. 63
  1. La Vision
 12. Barcarollette
 20. Petite marche villageoise
 13. Ressouvenir
 35. Musique militaire
 23. L'homme aux sabots
 31. Début de Quatuor
 39. Héraclite et Démocrite

Rotterdam, 12. Dezember 1902 (Erster Klavierabend!)

Etude F-dur op. 35,5 (Allegro barbaro)

Jean qui pleure et Jean qui rit, 2 Fugues da camera

Berlin 1903

Capriccio alla soldatesca op. 50

(Alkan)   J'étais endormie, mais mon cœur   } Dresden 1905
               veillait... (Cantique des canti-
               ques) (aus den 25 Préludes) op.
               31, 13

               Etude a-moll Comme le vent op. 39,1 ⎫

               Etude D-dur op. 35,2   ⎪

               Etude A-dur op. 35,1   ⎬ Manchester 1907

               Etude E-dur (Oktaven) op. 35,12   ⎭

               Etude d-moll Le chemin de fer op. 27   Manchester 1909

               Symphonie c-moll aus den Etudes
               mineures op. 39,4-7   Berlin 1910

               Prélude (Librement) op. 31,7   ⎫

               Prélude (La chanson de la folle au ⎪
               bord de la mer) op. 31,8   ⎬ Manchester 1911

               Prélude (Ancienne mélodie de la   ⎪
               synagogue) op. 31,6   ⎪

               Marche (quasi da cavalleria)   ⎪
               aus op. 37   ⎭

               Aus den Treize prières für Klavier ⎫
               zu drei Händen oder für Pedalflügel ⎪
               op. 64 (mit Charles Kelly an zwei   ⎪
               Klavieren)   ⎬ Manchester 1911
                   Nr. 4 B-dur   ⎪
                   Nr. 9 E-dur   ⎪
                   Nr.11 E-dur   ⎪
                   Nr.12 F-dur   ⎪
                   Nr. 8 B-dur (Dieu des armées)   ⎭

               Prélude (rapidement) op. 31,14   ⎫

               Prélude (modérément vite et bien   ⎬ Zakopane 1919
               caractérisé) op. 31,20   ⎭

Auber s. Liszt

Bach   Zwei Inventionen Es-dur, C-dur   Dresden 1892

               Italienisches Konzert   Dresden 1904

               Chromatische Phantasie (Busoni)   Manchester 1907

Bach	Präludien und Fugen aus dem Wohl-temperierten Klavier
	I. Teil
	    Nr. 22 b-moll
	    Nr. 13 Fis-dur
	    Nr. 5 D-dur
	II. Teil
	    Nr. 15 (39) G-dur
	    Nr. 7 (31) Es-dur
		Manchester 1909

	Zweistimmige Inventionen
	    Nr. 6 E-dur
	    Nr. 8 F-dur
		Manchester 1910

	Chromatische Phantasie und Fuge Toccata c-moll	Liverpool 1910
	Konzert c-moll für zwei Klaviere und Orchester (mit Else Baare unter Heinrich Schulz)	Warnemünde 1915
	Fantasie c-moll	Krakau 1916
Bach-Busoni	Toccata, Adagio und Fuge C-dur	Wiesbaden 1902

	Orgelchoralvorspiele
	    Wachet auf, ruft uns die Stimme
	    Nun freut euch, lieben Christen g'mein
	    Ich ruf zu dir, Herr Jesu Christ
	    In dir ist Freude
		Utrecht 1902

	Präludium und Fuge D-dur	Vlissingen 1903
	Chaconne	London 1903
	Toccata d-moll	Oldenburg 1906
	Präludium und Fuge Es-dur	Berlin 1911
	Konzert d-moll (unter Busoni)	Berlin 1914
	Präludium, Fuge und Allegro Es-dur (für das Lautenklavier) Capriccio über die Abreise des vielgeliebten Bruders	Dresden 1914
	Goldberg-Variationen	Zakopane 1918
	Choralvorspiel "Nun komm der Heiden Heiland"	Posen 1923
	Fantasia, Adagio e Fuga (c-moll)	Berlin 1924

5

Bach-Liszt	Präludium und Fuge a-moll	Leningrad	1927
Bach-Petri	Toccata c-moll	Zakopane(?)	1919
	Konzert und Fuge c-moll	Zakopane	1919
	Menuett	Zakopane	1919
	Toccata D-dur	Zakopane	1919
	Fantasie g-moll	Zakopane	1920
	Partita e-moll	Berlin	1922
	Fragment einer Suite f-moll	Leipzig	1923
	Fragment einer Suite A-dur	Berlin	1924
	Italienisches Konzert	Tiflis	1927
Balakirew	Islamey	Leningrad	1927
Beethoven	Sonate E-dur op. 109	Utrecht	1902
	32 Variationen c-moll	Berlin	1903
	Sonata appassionata op. 57	's-Gravenhage	1903
	Konzert für Klavier, Violine, Violoncello und Orchester op. 56 (mit Henri Petri und Georg Wille unter Adolf Hagen)	Dresden	1904
	Konzert Nr. 4 G-dur op. 58 (unter Wilhelm Schmidt)	Zwickau	1905
	Sonata quasi una fantasia Cis-dur op. 27,2	Manchester	1905
	Konzert Nr. 5 Es-dur op. 73 (unter Hans Richter)	Manchester	1905
	Sonate C-dur op. 53 (Waldstein)	Manchester	1906
	Sonate As-dur op. 26		
	Sonate Es-dur op. 27,1		
	Sonate D-dur op. 28		
	Sonate G-dur op. 31,1		
	Sonate d-moll op. 31,2		
	Sonate Es-dur op. 31,3		

6

(Beethoven)   Sonate F-dur op. 54

Sonate Fis-dur op. 78   ⎫
                                ⎪ Manchester 1908
Sonatine G-dur op. 79   ⎪

Sonate Es-dur op. 81a (Les adieux)

Sonate e-moll op. 90

Sonate A-dur op. 101

Sonate B-dur op. 106 (für das
                    Hammerklavier)

Sonate As-dur op. 110

Sonate c-moll op. 111

Sonate c-moll op. 13 (Pathétique)   Basel 1908

Sonate e-moll op. 2,1   ⎫

Sonate C-dur op. 2,3   ⎪

Sonate Es-dur op. 7   ⎬ Manchester 1908

Sonate g-moll op. 49,1   ⎪

Sonate F-dur op. 10,2   ⎪

Sonate D-dur op. 10,3   ⎭

Variationen op. 35 ("Eroica")   ⎫

Sechs Bagatellen op. 126   ⎬ Manchester 1909

Rondo a capriccio (Die Wut über
den verlorenen Groschen) op. 129 ⎭

Konzert Nr. 3 c-moll op. 37
(unter W. A. Brewerton)   Wilmslow 1909

Fantasie op. 77   Manchester 1911

Chorphantasie op. 80
(unter Michael Balling)   Manchester 1913

Andante F-dur   Rostock 1916

Konzert Nr. 2 B-dur op. 19   ⎫
(unter Max Fiedler)   ⎪
                              ⎬ Amsterdam 1920
Konzert Nr. 1 C-dur op. 15   ⎪
(unter Max Fiedler)   ⎭

Total : 26 Sonatas

7

Beethoven-Busoni	Ecossaisen	Manchester	1911
Beethoven-Liszt (s. a. Liszt)	Adelaide	Wiesbaden	1905
	Busslied	Manchester	1907
	2. Symphonie	Zakopane	1920
Beethoven-Tausig	Scherzo aus dem Quartett op.59,2	Zakopane	1918
Bellini s. Liszt			
Bizet s. Busoni			
Brahms (s.a. Gluck)	Konzert Nr. 1 d-moll op. 15 (unter Henri Wood)	London	1903
	Intermezzo Es-dur op. 117,1	London	1904
	Rhapsodie g-moll op. 79,2		
	Variationen und Fuge über ein Thema von Händel op. 24	Dresden	1905
	Paganini-Variationen op. 35 Heft I und II	Ashton	1908
	Sonate f-moll op. 5	Manchester	1909
	Sonate fis-moll op. 2	Manchester	1909
	Vier Balladen op. 10 Nr. 1 d-moll Nr. 2 D-dur Nr. 3 h-moll Nr. 4 H-dur	Manchester	1909
	Rhapsodie h-moll op. 79,1	Manchester	1910
	Variationen über ein Tema von Haydn für zwei Klaviere (mit Charles Kelly)	Manchester	1911
	Intermezzo b-moll op. 117,2	London	1912
	Intermezzo cis-moll op. 117,3	Manchester	1912
	Konzert Nr. 2 B-dur op. 83 unter H. P. Allen)	Oxford	1912
	Sechs Klavierstücke op. 118 Nr. 1 Intermezzo a-moll Nr. 2 Intermezzo A-dur Nr. 3 Ballade g-moll Nr. 4 Intermezzo f-moll Nr. 5 Romanze F-dur Nr. 6 Intermezzo Es-moll	Krakau	1918

8

Brahms-Busoni	3 Choralvorspiele aus op. 122		
	Nr. 3 Es ist ein Ros' entsprungen		
	Nr. 4 Herzlich tut mich verlangen	Manchester	1911
	Nr. 1 Herzlich tut mich erfreuen		
Busoni	Concerto op. XXXIX (unter Busoni)	Amsterdam	1905
(s. a. Bach,			
Beethoven,	Sechs Elegien	Manchester	1909
Brahms,			
Liszt,	Fantasia über Bachs "Christ, du		
Mozart)	bist der helle Tag" (auf den Tod	Berlin	1911
	seines Vaters)		
	Erste Sonatine		
	Fantasia contrappuntistica	Berlin	1912
	Preludio, Fuga e Fuga figurata	Berlin	1912
	(nach Bach)		
	Giga, Bolero e Variazione	Berlin	1912
	(nach Mozart)		
	Berceuse	Cambridge	1913
	Zwei kontrapunktische Tanzstücke		
	Nr. 1 Waffentanz	Dresden	1914
	Nr. 2 Friedenstanz		
	Indianische Fantasie op. 44	Berlin	1914
	(unter Busoni)		
	Indianisches Tagebuch	Dresden	1916
	Vierte Ballettszene (Walzer und		
	Galopp)	Krakau	1918
	Improvisation über das Bachsche		
	Chorallied "Wie wohl ist mir,		
	o Freund der Seelen" für zwei	Łodz	1920
	Klaviere (mit Karol Szreter)		
	Duettino concertante nach Mozart		
	für zwei Klaviere (mit Busoni)		
		Berlin	1921
	Fantasia contrappuntistica		
	für zwei Klaviere (mit Busoni)		
	Drei Albumblätter (Uraufführung)		
		Berlin	1922
	Toccata		
	Romanza e Scherzoso (unter Hermann	Frankfurt	1922
	v. Glenck)		

9

(Busoni)	Prélude et Etude en arpèges		
	Drei polyphone Stücke	Weimar	1923
	Perpetuum mobile		
	Zweite Sonatine	Berlin	1928
	Kammerfantasie über Carmen (Bizet)		
Casella	Partita (unter Henry Wood)	London	1928
Chopin · (s.a. Liszt, Hexameron)	Zwölf Etuden op. 10	Berlin	1903
	Nocturne H-dur op. 62,1	Berlin	1903
	Polonaise As-dur op. 53		
	Nocturne Fis-dur op. 15,2	Vlissingen	1903
	Ballade Nr. 1 g-moll op. 23		
	Nocturne Des-dur op. 27,2	London	1903
	Nocturne c-moll op. 48,1	Reading	1904
	Scherzo Nr. 2 b-moll op. 31	London	1906
	Berceuse op. 57	Bowdon	1906
	6 Préludes aus op. 28	Bradford	1907
	Impromptu Nr. 2 Fis-dur op. 36	's-Gravenhage (Privatkonzert d. Königin)	1907
	Valse	Manchester	1908
	Ballade Nr. 4 f-moll op. 52	Ashton	1908
	Scherzo Nr. 3 cis-moll op. 39		
	Sonate Nr. 3 h-moll op. 58	Dresden	1908
	24 Préludes op. 28 (das Gesamtwerk)		
	Barcarolle op. 60		
	Ballade Nr. 3 As-dur op. 47	Ashton	1908
	Sonate Nr. 2 b-moll op. 35	Manchester	1909
	Ballade Nr. 2 F-dur op. 38	Manchester	1909
	Fantaisie f-moll op. 49	Manchester	1909
	Variations brillantes ("Je vends des scapulaires") op. 12	Manchester	1909

(Chopin)	Aus den Etuden op. 25 Nr. 1 As-dur Nr. 2 f-moll Nr. 3 F-dur Nr. 9 Ges-dur Nr. 11 a-moll	Manchester	1909
	Valse As-dur (op. 34,1 oder op. 42?)	Manchester	1910
	Polonaise fis-moll op. 44	Berlin	1912
	Zwölf Etuden op. 25 (das Gesamtwerk)	Berlin	1912
	Nocturne Es-dur op. 55,2	Deansgate	1913
	Polonaise-Fantaisie op. 61	Dresden	1913
	Nocturne cis-moll op. 27,1	London	1913
	Nocturne G-dur op. 37,2	Dresden	1914
	Impromptu Nr. Ges-dur op. 51 Scherzo Nr. 1 h-moll op. 20	Berlin	1915
	Konzert Nr. 2 f-moll op. 21 (unter Emil Młynarski)	Warschau	1920
	Nocturne E-dur op. 62	Zakopane	1929
Czerny s. Liszt, Hexameron			
Debussy	Aus den Préludes I Nr. 8 La fille aux cheveux de lin Nr. 5 Les collines d'Anacapri Nr. 10 La cathédrale engloutie Nr. 12 Minstrels	Zakopane	1919
	En blanc et noir für zwei Klaviere (mit Karol Szreter)	Łodz	1920
	Trois pièces für zwei Klaviere (mit Leo Sirota)	Moskau	1925
	Reflets dans l'eau (Images I,1) Feux d'Artifice (Préludes II,12)	Krakau	1926
	La sérenade interrompue (Préludes I,9)	Warsaw Warschau	1926
Donizetti s. Liszt			
Franck	Prélude, Choral et Fugue	Rotterdam	1902
	Prélude, Aria et Final	Manchester	1910

(Franck)	Variations symphoniques (unter Hans Richter)	Manchester	1911
	Les Djinns (unter H. P, Allen)	Oxford	1912
Glasunow	Drei Klavierstücke op. 49	Berlin	1923
Gluck-Brahms	Gavotte (aus Paride ed Elena)	Manchester	1910
Gluck-Saint=Saëns	Alceste, Caprice sur les Airs de Ballet	Zakopane	1919
Gluck-Sgambati	Mélodie (d'Orphée)	Łwow	1929
Gounod-Liszt	Faust-Walzer	Manchester	1907
Haydn	Sonate Nr. 7 D-dur, zweiter und erster Satz	Dresden,29.Juli 1891 (Erstes Auftreten!)	

Variationen f-moll

Sonate Es-dur   } Manchester 1909

Henselt

Etude As-dur op. 5,6 (Danklied nach Sturm)

Etude Fis-dur op. 2,6 (Si oiseau j'étais)   } Manchester 1909

Etude D-dur op. 2,7 (C'est la jeunesse, qui a des ailes dorées)

Etude e-moll op. 2,10 (Comme le ruisseau)

Etude A-dur op. 5,9   } Manchester 1909

Herz s. Liszt, Hexameron

Liszt (s.a. Bach, Beethoven, Gounod, Mendelssohn, Meyerbeer, Rossini, Schubert, Wagner)

Variationen über "Weinen, Klagen" (Bach)

Sechs Paganini-Etuden
    Nr. 1 g-moll (Tremolo)
    Nr. 2 Es-dur (Andantino capriccioso)
    Nr. 3 gis-moll (La campanella)   } Rotterdam 1902
    Nr. 4 E-dur (Arpeggio)
    Nr. 5 E-dur (La chasse)
    Nr. 6 a-moll (Tema con variazioni)

Réminiscences de Lucrezia Borgia (Donizetti)

12

(Liszt)	Drei Petrarca-Sonette (Années de pèlerinage II,4-6) 　Sonett 47 Des-dur 　Sonett 104 E-dur 　Sonett 123 As-dur	Berlin	1903
	Konzert Nr. 2 A-dur (unter Willem Mengelberg)	Amsterdam	1903
	Au bord d'une source (Années de pèlerinage I,4) Rigoletto-Fantasie (Verdi)	Vlissingen	1903
	Fantasie über Ungarische Volksmelodien 　　(unter Henry Wood)	London	1904
	Polonaise Nr. 2 E-dur	Blankenberg	1904
	Heroischer Marsch im Ungarischen Styl 　　　　　　　　(Busoni)	Bradford	1905
	Concert pathétique für zwei Klaviere 　　(mit Busoni)	Amsterdam	1905
	Les jeux d'eaux à la Villa d'Este (Années de pèlerinage II,4) Légende Nr. II St. François de Paule marchant sur les flots	Wiesbaden	1905
	Sposalizio (Années de pèlerinage II,1)	Manchester	1905
	Ungarische Rhapsodie Nr. 9 (Pesther 　　　　　　　　　Carneval)	Lincoln	1906
	Valse de concert sur deux motifs de Lucia e Parisina (Donizetti)	Manchester	1906
	Légende Nr. I St. François d'Assise. La prédication aux oiseaux	London	1906
	Etude Waldesrauschen	Bowdon	1906
	Tarantella di bravura (Auber)	Bradford	1907
	Ungarische Rhapsodie Nr. 13	Manchester	1908
	Ungarische Rhapsodie Nr. 8	Ashton	1908
	Fantasie über Beethovens Ruinen von Athen (unter Busoni)	Berlin	1908

13

(Liszt)	Sonate h-moll		
	Réminiscences de Don Juan (Mozart) für zwei Klaviere (mit Busoni)	Berlin	1908
	Bénédiction de Dieu dans la solitude (Harmonies poétiques et religieuses Nr. 3)		
	Ungarische Rhapsodie Nr. 12		
	Ungarische Rhapsodie Nr. 5 (Héroide-élégiaque)	Manchester	1909
	Ungarische Rhapsodie Nr. 2		
	Etude Gnomenreigen	Manchester	1909
	Phantasie und Fuge über den Namen B-a-c-h	Manchester	1909
	Ballade Nr. II h-moll	Manchester	1909
	H e x a m e r o n , Variationen über den Puritaner-Marsch (Bellini) (von Liszt, Thalberg, Pixis, Herz, Czerny und Chopin)	Manchester	1909
	Etudes d'exécution transcendante Nr. 5 Feux-follets Nr. 4 Mazeppa	Manchester	1909
	Apparition Nr. I	Berlin	1909
	Liebestraum Nr. 3	Manchester	1910
	Etude de concert Nr. 3 Des-dur	Pendleton	1910
	Polonaise Nr. II E-dur (mit Schluss-kadenz von Busoni)	Manchester	1910
	Somnambula-Fantasie (Bellini)	Manchester	1910
	Todtentanz (unter Hans Richter)	Manchester	1911
	Konzert Nr. I Es-dur (unter W. B. Brierley)	West Kirby	1911
	Chapelle de Guilleaume Tell (Années de pèlerinage I,1)		
	Canzonetta del Salvator Rosa (Années de pèlerinage II,3)	Berlin	1911
	Orage (Années de pèlerinage I,5)		

(Liszt)	Années de pèlerinage, Ire Année: La Suisse (ganz) Valse mélancolique	Dresden	1911
	Années de pèlerinage, IIme Année: L'Italie und Supplement: Venezia e Napoli (ganz) Die Trauergondel En rêve	Dresden	1912
	Années de pèlerinage, IIIme Année (ganz) Polonaise Nr. I c-moll	Dresden	1912
	Valse a capriccio sur deux motifs de Lucia e Parisina (Donizetti) (Erste Ausgabe)	Dresden	1913
	Réminiscences de Don Juan (Mozart)	Oxford	1913
	Aus dem "Weihnachtsbaum" Altprovenzalisches Weihnachtslied Die Hirten an der Krippe Ungarisch Wiegenlied Carillon Polnisch	Berlin	1914
	Rhapsodie espagnole	Zakopane	1921
	Etudes d'exécution transcendante Nr. 10 f-moll Nr. 7 Eroica Es-dur Nr. 11 Harmonies du soir Des-dur	Moskau	1924
	Douze Etudes d'exécution transcendante (das Gesamtwerk)	Lwów	1927
Liszt-Busoni	Rhapsodie espagnole (unter Henry Wood)	London	1903
	Mephisto-Walzer	Manchester	1906
	Phantasie und Fuge über den Choral "Ad nos, ad salutarem undam" (aus Meyerbeers Le Prophète)	Berlin	1911
	Fantasie über zwei Motive aus Mozarts Oper Le nozze di Figaro	Berlin	1912
Medtner	Deux Contes b-moll und h-moll op. 20	Zakopane	1926

Mendelssohn	Lieder ohne Worte Nr. 1 E-dur op. 19,1 Nr. 30 A-dur op. 62,2 (Frühlingslied) Nr. 18 As-dur op. 38,6 (Duett) Nr. 34 C-dur op. 67,4 (Spinnerlied) Variations sérieuses op. 54	Manchester	1909
	Phantasie fis-moll op. 28	Manchester	1909
Mendelssohn-Liszt	Hochzeitsmarsch und Elfen- reigen (aus dem Sommernachts- traum)	Goslar	1908
Meyerbeer-Liszt (s. a. Liszt)	Illustrationen aus Le Prophète Nr. 2 Les patineurs. Scherzo	Midland	1907
Mozart	Fantasie d-moll (K.-V. 397)	Dresden	1892
	Konzert Nr. 20 d-moll (K.-V. 466) (mit Kadenzen von Busoni) (unter Busoni)	Berlin	1908
	Fantasie c-moll (K.-V. 475) Sonate A-dur (K.-V. 331)	Manchester	1909
	Konzert Nr. 23 A-dur (K.-V. 488) (unter Paul Hein)	Baden-Baden	1912
	Sonate D-dur für zwei Klaviere (K.-V. 448) (mit Karol Szreter)	Łodz	1920
	Konzert Nr. 17 G-dur (K.-V. 453) (mit Kadenzen von Busoni) (unter Emil Młynarski)	Warschau	1922
	Konzert Nr. 22 Es-dur (K.-V. 482) (mit Kadenzen von Busoni) (unter Walerjan Berdiajew)	Łodz	1923
	Konzert Nr. 24 c-moll (K.-V. 491) (mit Kadenzen von Busoni) (unter Henry Wood)	London	1926
	Konzert Nr. 19 F-dur (K.-V. 459) (mit Kadenzen von Busoni) (unter Henry Wood)	London	1929
	Konzert Es-dur für zwei Klaviere und Orchester (K.-V. 365) (mit Kadenzen von Petri) (mit Karol Szreter unter Michael Taube)	Berlin	1929

16

Mozart-Busoni	Andantino aus dem 9. Klavierkonzert (K.-V. 271)	Berlin	1916
	Fantasie für eine Orgelwalze (K.-V. 608) für zwei Klaviere (mit Busoni)	London	1922
	Ständchen aus Don Giovanni	Berlin	1924
	Ouverture zur Zauberflöte für zwei Klaviere (mit Michael v. Zadora)	Berlin	1924
Paganini s. Liszt			
Petri (s. a. Bach)	Zwei Klavierstücke 1.Am Bache 2.Scherzo	Dresden	1894
	Konzertstück c-moll op. 2 für Klavier und Orchester (unter Henry Wood)	London	1906
Pixis s. Liszt, Hexameron			
Prokofieff	Dritte Sonate a-moll op. 28 (d'après des vieux cahiers)	Leningrad	1927
	Toccata d-moll op. 11		
	Gavotta fis-moll op. 32,3	Zakopane	1928
	Marsch aus der Oper Die drei Orangen		
	Prélude C-dur op. 12,7 (?)	Warschau	1929
Rachmaninoff	Zweite Suite für zwei Klaviere op. 17 (?) (mit Leo Sirota)	Charków	1925
	Erste Suite für zwei Klaviere op. 5 (?) (mit Leo Sirota)	Moskau	1925
	Zwei Préludes G-dur und g-moll	Zakopane	1926
	Prélude d-moll	Redhill	1928
	Prélude es-moll	London	1929
Ravel	Sonatina	Krakau	1926
	Jeux d'eaux	Mailand	1928
	Pavane pour une infahte défunte	Zakopane	1926

Reger	Variationen über ein Thema von Beethoven, für zwei Klaviere op. 86 (mit Max Mayer)	Manchester 1910
Rossini-Liszt	La Serenata. Notturno (Soirées musicales Nr. 10)	Manchester 1906
Rubinstein	Etude C-dur (auf den falschen Ton)	Manchester 1909
	Thema und Variationen G-dur op. 88	Manchester 1909
Saint-Saëns (s.a. Glück)	Konzert Nr. 5 F-dur op. 103 (unter	Groningen 1904
	Variationen über ein Thema von Beethoven, für zwei Klaviere op. 35 (mit Max Mayer)	Manchester 1910
	Scherzo für zwei Klaviere (mit Charles Kelly)	Manchester 1911
	Polonaise für zwei Klaviere (mit Charles Kelly)	
Scarlatti-Tausig	Pastorale und Capriccio	Manchester 1910
Schubert	Quatre Impromptus op. 90	London 1904
	Phantasie C-dur op. 15 (Wanderer-Phantasie)	Manchester 1907
	Sonate B-dur (posth.)	Manchester 1909
	Impromptu B-dur op. 142,3 (Thema mit Variationen)	Manchester 1909
	Vier Moments musicaux aus op. 94 Nr. 3 f-moll Nr. 4 cis-moll Nr. 5 f-moll Nr. 6 As-dur	Zakopane 1928
Schubert-Liszt	Erlkönig	Bowdon 1906
	Wanderer-Phantasie (unter Olsen)	Dresden 1907
	Liebesbotschaft	
	Die Forelle	
	Gretchen am Spinnrad	Berlin 1912

18

(Schubert-Liszt)	Der Lindenbaum		
	Auf dem Wasser zu singen		
	Ständchen von Shakespeare	Berlin	1917
	Soirée de Vienne Nr. 6	Leningrad	1925
	Soirée de Vienne Nr. 5	Rostow	1925
Schubert-Tausig	Militärmarsch Des-dur	Reading	1904
	Andante und Variationen h-moll	Deansgate	1913
	Rondo über französische Motive e-moll	Dresden	1913
Schumann	Romanze Fis-dur op. 28,2	's-Gravenhage (Privatkonzert der Königin)	1905
	Abegg-Variationen op. 1	London	1905
	Novellette F-dur op. 21,1	Manchester	1908
	Kreisleriana, acht Fantasien op. 16	Manchester	1909
	Toccata C-dur op. 7		
	Sonate Nr. 1 fis-moll op. 11	Manchester	1909
	Fantasie C-dur op. 17	Manchester	1909
	Aus den Fantasiestücken op. 12 Nr. 1 Des Abends Nr. 2 Aufschwung	Manchester	1910
	Klavierkonzert a-moll op. 54 (unter Hermann Kutzschbach)	Zwickau	1910
	Aus den Fantasiestücken op. 12 Nr. 5 In der Nacht Nr. 7 Traumeswirren	Rostock	1916
	Fantasiestücke op. 12 (das Gesamtwerk)	Zakopane	1917
	Papillons, zwölf Klavierstücke op. 2	Zakopane	1918

19

(Schumann)	Faschingsschwank aus Wien op.26	Berlin	1923
	Etudes en forme de variations (Etudes symphoniques)op.13	Moskau	1924
	Carnaval op. 9	Rostow	1925
Skrjabin	Sonate Nr. 4 Fis-dur op. 30		
	Aus den Zwölf Etuden op. 8 Nr. 1 Cis-dur (oder Nr. 12 Dis-dur?) Nr. 5 E-dur Nr. 8 As-dur Nr. 10 Des-dur	Leningrad	1927

Sgambati s. Gluck

Strauss-Tausig	"Man lebt nur einmal", Walzer	Leningrad	1925
Strawinskij	Aus Petruschka Russischer Tanz Bei Petruschka Karneval	Zakopane	1926

Tausig
s. Beethoven,
    Schubert,
    Strauss

Thalberg, s. Liszt, Hexameron

Tschaikowskij	Konzert Nr. 1 b-moll op. 23 (unter Henry Wood)	London	1903
Wagner-Liszt	Spinnerlied aus dem Fliegenden Holländer	Bologna	1914
Weber	Rondeau brillant Es-dur op. 62	London	1905
	Konzertstück f-moll op. 79 (unter G. H. Bennett)	Lincoln	1906
	Sonate As-dur op. 39	Bowdon	1909
	Aufforderung zum Tanz	Manchester	1909
	Sonate d-moll op. 49	Manchester	1909

20

Kammermusik

(mit Ausnahme der Liederbegleitungen)

d'Ambrosio	Canzonetta für Violine und Klavier (mit Henriette Terkühle)	Vlissingen	1903
Bach	Konzert E-dur für Violine und Klavier arr. (mit Issay Barmas)	Berlin	1903
	Sonate E-dur für Violine und Klavier (mit Mary Hall)	Birmingham	1904
	Sonate f-moll für Violine und Klavier (mit Adolph Brodsky)	Manchester	1911
Beethoven	Sonate A-dur (Kreutzer-Sonate) für Violine und Klavier op. 47 (mit Henri Petri)	Halle	1899
	Klaviertrio Es-dur op. 70,2 (mit Henri Petri und Georg Wille)	Dresden	1899
	Sonate A-dur op. 69 für Violoncello und Klavier (mit Georg Wille)	Halle	1902
	Romanze für Violine und Klavier arr. (mit Oliveira)	Anklam	1904
	Sonate c-moll op. 30,2 für Violine und Klavier (mit Marie Hall)	Swansea	1905
	Klaviertrio c-moll op. 1,3 (mit Adolph Brodsky und Carl Fuchs)	Manchester	1906
	Sonate D-dur op. 102,3 für Violoncello und Klavier (mit Julius Klengel)	Manchester	1909
	Klaviertrio D-dur op. 70,1 (mit Adolph Brodsky und Carl Fuchs)	Manchester	1909
	Sonate G-dur op. 30,3 für Violine und Klavier (mit Adolph Brodsky)	Manchester	1912
	Sonate F-dur op. 24 für Violine und Klavier (mit Henri Petri)	Grossenhain	1914
	Klaviertrio B-dur op. 97 (mit Franz Veit und Arnold Földesy)	Berlin	1915
	Sonate Es-dur op. 12,3 für Violine und Klavier (mit Josef Wolfsthal)	San Sebastian	1929

Brahms	Klavierquartett A-dur op. 26 (mit Henri Petri, Bernhard Unkenstein und Georg Wille)	Halle	1899
	Sonate Nr. 3 d-moll op. 108 für Violine und Klavier (mit Henri Petri)	Dresden	1899
	Klavierquintett f-moll op. 34 (mit Henri Petri, ..., Alfred Spitzner und Georg Wille)	Dresden	1900
	Klavierquartett g-moll op. 25 (mit Arno Hilf, Bernhard Unkenstein und Georg Wille)	Halle	1902
	Sonate Nr. 1 G-dur op. 78 für Violine und Klavier (mit Adolph Brodsky)	Manchester	1912
Busoni	Sonate Nr. 2 e-moll op. 36a für Violine und Klavier (mit Henri Petri)	Wiesbaden	1902
	Kultaselle. Zehn Variationen über ein finnisches Volkslied für Violoncello und Klavier (mit Julius Klengel)	Manchester	1909
Chopin	Introduction, Polonaise brillante c-moll op. 3 für Violoncello und Klavier (mit Carl Fuchs)	Manchester	1906
Corelli	La folia für Violine und Klavier (mit Joseph Szigeti)	Charkow	1925
Dvorak	Klaviertrio (Dumky) e-moll op. 90 (mit Carl Halir und Julius Klengel)	Bowdon	1909
Franck	Sonate A-dur für Violine und Klavier (mit Dorothy Bridson)	London	1903
	Klavierquintett f-moll (mit Adolph Brodsky, Rawdon C. Briggs, Simon Speelman und Carl Fuchs)	Bradford	1907
Goldmark	Suite für Violine und Klavier 2. und 3. Satz (mit Arthur Catterall)	Bradford	1908
Graener	Sonate E-dur für Violine und Klavier (mit Gustav Havemann)	Dresden	1921

22

Grieg	Sonate op. 36 für Violoncello und Klavier (mit Georg Wille)	Dresden	1921
	Sonate F-dur op. 8 für Violine und Klavier (mit Arthur Catterall)	Bradford	1909
	Sonate c-moll op. 45 für Violine und Klavier, erster Satz (mit Antonio de Grassi)	Middlesbrough	1912
Hauser	Ungarische Rhapsodie für Violine und Klavier (mit Henriette Terkühle)	Vlissingen	1903
Lehmann,Liza	Romantische Suite für Violine und Klavier (mit Ethel Barns)	London	1903
Mendelssohn	Klaviertrio d-moll op. 49 (mit Henri Petri und Georg Wille)	Dresden	1900
	Klaviertrio c-moll op. 66 (mit Jan Wolanek und Juro Tkalčič)	Zakopane	1917
Mozart	Sonate A-dur für Violine und Klavier (K.-V. 526) (mit Marie Hall)	Reading	1904
	Konzert D-dur (K.-V. 218) für Violine und Klavier arr. (mit Kocian Jorosłáw)	Zakopane	1916
	Sonate B-dur für Violine und Klavier (K.-V. 454) (mit Gustav Havemann)	Rostock	1916
Nschez	Romanze für Violine und Klavier (mit Henriette Terkühle)	Vlissingen	1903
Paganini	Variationen über Nel cor più non mi sento (Paesiello) für Violine und Klavier arr. (mit Jan Wolanek)	Zakopane	1920
Reger	Suite im alten Stil op. 93 für Violine und Klavier (mit Ernst Schiever)	Liverpool	1909
Ries	Larghetto aus dem Konzert für Violine und Klavier (arr.) (mit Henriette Terkühle)	Vlissingen	1903
Rosenbloom	Sonate c-moll für Violine und Klavier (mit Anton Maaskoff)	Manchester (?)	1911

Saint-Saëns	Klaviertrio F-dur op. 18 (mit Max Mossel und Johann C. Hock)	Dublin	1903
Schönberg	Pierrot Lunaire op. 28 (mit Elfriede John, Rezitation; Hendrik de Vries, Flöte; Gustav Havemann, Violine; Adolf Steiner, Violoncello; Woldemar Conrad, Klarinette; unter Hermann Scherchen)	Berlin	1922
Schubert	Klaviertrio Es-dur op. 100 (mit Hans Kötscher und Willy Treichler)	Basel	1904
	Rondeau brillant h-moll op.70 für Violine und Klavier (mit Adolph Brodsky)	Manchester	1906
	Klaviertrio B-dur op. 99 (mit Carl Halir und Julius Klengel)	Bowdon	1909
	Sonate A-dur op. 162 für Violine und Klavier (mit Alfred Wittenberg)	Berlin	1913
	Fantasie C-dur op. 159 für Violine und Klavier (mit Alfred Wittenberg)		
Schumann	Klaviertrio d-moll op. 63 (mit Henri Petri und Georg Wille)	Dresden	1899
	Klavierquartett Es-dur op. 47 (mit Henri Petri, Alfred Spitzner und Georg Wille)	Zwickau	1910
	Sonate Nr. 1 a-moll op. 105 für Violine und Klavier (mit Fritz Hirt)	Basel	1920
	Sonate Nr. 2 d-moll op. 121 für Violine und Klavier (mit Joseph Szigeti)	Charków	1925
Sinding	Suite a-moll op. 14 für Violine und Klavier (mit Henri Petri)	Wiesbaden	1902
Spohr	Adagio aus dem 9. Violinkonzert op. 55 für Violine und Klavier arr. (mit Adolph Brodsky)	Manchester	1912

(Spohr)	Adagio und Finale aus dem 7. Violinkonzert op. 38 für Violine und Klavier arr. (mit Henri Petri)	Grossenhain	1914
Strawinskij	Pergolese-Suite für Violine und Klavier arr. (mit Josef Wolfsthal)	Madrid	1929
Svendsen	Romanze G-dur für Violine und Klavier arr. (mit Issay Barmas)	Berlin	1903
Tenaglia(-Ries)	Aria (Begl'occhi mercè!) für Violine und Klavier arr. (mit Issay Barmas)	Berlin	1903
Tschaikowskij	Scherzo aus op. 42 (Souvenir d'un lieu cher) für Violine und Klavier (mit Issay Barmas)	Berlin	1903
	Klaviertrio a-moll op. 50 (mit Max Mossel und Johann C. Hock)	Dublin	1903
Vieuxtemps	Ballade und Polonaise für Violine und Klavier arr. (mit Henri Petri)	Grossenhain	1914
Vitali	Konzert für Violine und Klavier arr. (mit Joseph Szigeti)	Charków	1925
Wieniawski	Mazurka Nr. 1 für Violine und Klavier (mit Henriette Terkühle)	Vlissingen	1903
	Tarantelle für Violine und Klavier (mit Oliveira)	Anklam	1904

About the Author

Dr. Alfred O. Kanwischer holds a Bachelor of Music from Heidelberg University and a Doctor of Musical Arts from Boston University, where he was a member of the distinguished piano faculty for eleven years. He is currently Professor Emeritus at San José State University's School of Music in California.

He has given lectures, lecture-recitals, master classes, and under-graduate and graduate seminars at Boston University, Harvard University, the Berkshire Music Festival, the Tanglewood Festival, Sun-river Music Festival in Oregon, the College Music Society, and the American Beethoven Society. He ran the Peabody Piano Seminars at Peabody College for Teachers in Nashville, Tennessee, and, together with his wife, Heidi, created the John Ringling Festival Concerts in Sarasota, Florida.

His scholarly articles, focusing especially on Bach, Beethoven, and Brahms, have appeared in the *American Music Teacher*, the Music Teachers Association journals in Massachusetts, Connecticut, Tennessee, and California; in the journal of the American Liszt Society; and the *Beethoven Journal*. These include analyses of Beethoven's Op. 2/1, Op. 53, and Op. 110, and a study of Beethoven's Erard piano.

Dr. Kanwischer has concertized throughout the United States, Canada, Europe, and Asia, giving both solo concerts and duo-piano concerts with his wife, Heidi Elfenbein Kanwischer, whom he met in San

Francisco when they were both pupils of Egon Petri. Concert venues include Lincoln Center, New York; Jordan Hall, Boston; Herbst Theatre, San Francisco; Wigmore Hall, London; the Concertgebouw, Amsterdam; de Doolen, Rotterdam; as well as venues in Munich, Salzburg, Seoul, and Tokyo. Broadcasts include the BBC, London; WBUR, Boston; WQXR, New York; KPFA, Berkeley; and WGBH, Boston, among others. The Kanwischers were with Albert Kay Concert Artists Management, New York, for twenty-five years. They have recorded for Orion and United Sound.

Dr. Kanwischer, a pupil of Egon Petri and Bela Nagy, is highly regarded as a master teacher of music history, theory, and performance. His students have gone on to study at the Juilliard School of Music, Indiana University, and Curtis Institute, among other distinguished institutions, and become teachers, professors, and performers throughout the United States, Canada, and Asia. Although he now resides near his daughter, Sylvia, and son-in-law in North Carolina, students still come to him from all parts of the United States for coaching. With an occasional concert or lecture on his schedule, he currently devotes most of his time to writing.

His book, *From Bach's Goldberg to Beethoven's Diabelli,* was published by Rowman and Littlefield in 2014.

Lightning Source UK Ltd.
Milton Keynes UK
UKHW041052080719
345787UK00009B/2597/P